MASTERING
C++ PROGRAMMING FOR GUI DEVELOPMENT WITH QT

ETHAN D. RYDER

A STEP BY STEP GUIDE TO BUILDING CROSS-PLATFORM GUI APPLICATIONS WITH C++ AND QT FRAMEWORK

Table of content

Table of content..2
DISCLAIMER..6
INTRODUCTION..8
Part I: Getting Started with Qt 6........................14
  Chapter 1: Installing and Setting Up Qt 6........15
    Choosing the Right Qt Components...........19
    Configuring Qt Creator................................23
    Creating Your First Qt Project....................27
  Chapter 2: Essential C++ Concepts for Qt......32
    Classes, Objects, and Inheritance.............39
    Memory Management with Smart Pointers 44
    Lambda Expressions and the Standard Library..49
    Error Handling and Exception Handling.....54
  Chapter 3: Building Your First Qt GUI Application..59
    Designing the User Interface with Qt Designer...63
    Laying Out Widgets with Layouts...............67
    Connecting Signals and Slots....................71
    Compiling and Running Your Application...76
Part II: Mastering Qt Core Concepts.................80
  Chapter 4: Signals and Slots: The Heart of Qt Communication..81
    Custom Signals and Slots..........................85

Connecting Signals and Slots Programmatically..................91

Advanced Signal-Slot Techniques............96

Chapter 5: Layouts: Organizing Your GUI..... 102

Custom Layouts...................................... 106

Responsive Design with Layouts.............110

Best Practices for Layout Management....114

Chapter 6: Widgets: The Building Blocks of Your GUI... 120

Custom Widgets...................................... 124

Styling Widgets with Stylesheets..............129

Accessibility and Widgets........................ 135

Chapter 7: QML: Declarative UI Design......... 140

QML Syntax and Basic Elements.............144

Integrating QML with C++....................... 149

Building Dynamic UIs with QML............... 156

Part III: Advanced Qt Techniques..................... 162

Chapter 8: Model-View Architecture: Structuring Your Data.. 163

Built-in Qt Models..................................... 167

Creating Custom Models......................... 173

Data Visualization with Views................... 178

Chapter 9: Database Integration: Connecting to Your Data.. 185

Connecting to Databases........................ 190

Executing Queries and Retrieving Data... 196

Displaying Data in Your GUI.....................201

Chapter 10: Networking: Communicating with the World.. 208
- Making HTTP Requests......................... 213
- TCP and UDP Communication.................219
- Building Networked Applications............. 225

Chapter 11: Multithreading: Enhancing Performance... 231
- QThread and Worker Objects.................. 236
- Synchronizing Threads............................241
- Best Practices for Multithreaded Applications 247

Chapter 12: 3D Graphics with Qt 3D............. 252
- Creating 3D Scenes................................ 256
- Animating and Interacting with 3D Objects.... 262
- Integrating 3D Graphics in Your GUI........ 269

Chapter 13: Qt Quick: Building Fluid UIs........ 275
- Qt Quick Controls................................... 281
- Animations and Transitions...................... 287
- Building Touch-friendly Interfaces............ 293

Part IV: Real-world Projects................................ 299

Chapter 14: Building a Cross-platform Media Player..300
- Designing the User Interface....................305
- Implementing Media Playback................. 309
- Cross-platform Considerations..................314

Chapter 15: Developing a Custom Image Editor.

319

    Image Manipulation with Qt......................324

    Designing the Editor Interface..................331

    Implementing Editing Features.................335

Chapter 16: Creating a Networked Chat Application.. 344

    Client-Server Architecture........................ 350

    Implementing Chat Functionality..............354

    Handling User Authentication...................359

Part V: Best Practices and Beyond................ 363

Chapter 17: Coding Standards and Design Patterns... 364

    Design Patterns for Qt Development........370

    Writing Clean and Maintainable Code......376

Chapter 18: Troubleshooting and Debugging 381

    Debugging Techniques............................387

    Qt Test Framework.................................. 392

Chapter 19: Building Your Qt Developer Career.. 398

    Preparing for Interviews........................... 402

    Navigating the Job Market.......................407

Glossary of Key Teams................................412

DISCLAIMER

The information provided in this book, "C++ Programming for GUI Development with Qt: A Comprehensive Guide," is intended for educational and informational purposes only. While every effort has been made to ensure the accuracy and completeness of the content, the authors and publisher make no representations or warranties of any kind, express or implied, about the completeness, accuracy, reliability, suitability, or availability of the information, code examples, or graphics contained within this book.

The use of the information and code examples in this book is at your own risk. The authors and publisher shall not be liable for any errors, omissions, or any losses, injuries, or damages arising from the use of this information.

This book is not a substitute for professional advice or training. If you require specific guidance or assistance with Qt development, it is recommended that you consult with a qualified professional.

The technologies, tools, and versions mentioned in this book are subject to change and updates. It is your responsibility to ensure that you are using the most current versions and practices.

Some of the code examples in this book might require additional libraries or dependencies. It is your responsibility to ensure that you have the necessary components installed and configured correctly.

The authors and publisher do not endorse any specific third-party products, services, or websites mentioned in this book. Any references to such entities are for informational purposes only.

By using this book, you agree to the terms of this disclaimer. If you do not agree with any part of this disclaimer, you should not use this book.

INTRODUCTION

In the realm of software development, where functionality intertwines with aesthetics, lies the art of crafting graphical user interfaces (GUIs). A well-designed GUI not only empowers users to interact seamlessly with your application but also leaves a lasting impression of professionalism and polish. If you're a C++ programmer seeking to elevate your skills in GUI development, Qt emerges as a powerful and versatile toolkit that can turn your vision into reality.

Qt is a cross-platform framework renowned for its flexibility, enabling you to create stunning GUIs that run seamlessly on major operating systems like Windows, macOS, and Linux. This inherent portability eliminates the need to rewrite code for each platform, saving you valuable time and effort. Qt's extensive library of pre-built widgets, coupled with its intuitive signal-slot mechanism, streamlines the development process, empowering you to craft visually appealing and interactive interfaces with remarkable efficiency.

Furthermore, Qt's declarative language, QML, opens the door to a world of dynamic and fluid user experiences. By combining the power of C++ with the expressiveness of QML, you gain the ability to build modern, touch-friendly interfaces that captivate and engage users. Whether you're developing desktop applications, embedded systems, or even mobile apps, Qt provides the tools and capabilities to bring your creative ideas to life.

Why Choose Qt for C++ GUI Development?

Among the multitude of GUI development frameworks available, Qt stands out for several compelling reasons. Its cross-platform nature ensures that your applications reach a wider audience, maximizing their impact and potential. The framework's rich feature set, including widgets, layouts, multimedia support, and networking capabilities, equips you with the building blocks to construct sophisticated and feature-rich GUIs. Qt's performance and efficiency are noteworthy; its optimized code and underlying architecture deliver responsive and fluid user experiences even on resource-constrained devices.

Qt also boasts a vibrant and supportive community, where developers of all skill levels share knowledge, collaborate on projects, and provide assistance. The abundance of online resources, tutorials, and documentation further accelerates the learning process, empowering you to overcome challenges and expand your Qt expertise.

Target Audience and Prerequisites

This book is tailored for C++ programmers who aspire to master the art of GUI development using Qt. Whether you're a novice programmer venturing into the world of GUIs or an experienced developer seeking to harness Qt's capabilities, this book will guide you on your journey. While prior experience with C++ is beneficial, we assume no prior knowledge of Qt or GUI development. Our focus is on providing clear explanations, practical examples, and hands-on exercises that gradually build your understanding and proficiency.

How to Use This Book

This book is structured to facilitate a step-by-step learning process, beginning with the fundamentals of Qt and gradually progressing to advanced techniques and real-world projects. Each chapter builds upon the knowledge gained in previous chapters, ensuring a smooth and logical progression. We encourage you to actively engage with the material by following along with the code examples, experimenting with the concepts, and completing the exercises provided.

The book is organized into five distinct parts:

- **Part I: Getting Started with Qt 6:** This part lays the foundation for your Qt journey, covering the installation and setup process, essential C++ concepts relevant to Qt development, and the creation of your first Qt GUI application.
- **Part II: Mastering Qt Core Concepts:** Here, we delve into the core concepts that underpin Qt development, including signals and slots, layouts, widgets, and QML. You'll gain a deep understanding of these fundamental building blocks and learn how to wield them effectively to craft visually appealing and interactive interfaces.
- **Part III: Advanced Qt Techniques:** This part explores advanced Qt techniques, such as the Model-View architecture, database integration, networking, multithreading, 3D graphics, and Qt Quick. By mastering these techniques, you'll be equipped to build sophisticated applications that handle complex data, communicate with external systems, and deliver captivating user experiences.
- **Part IV: Real-World Projects:** In this part, we put theory into practice by guiding you

through the development of three real-world projects: a cross-platform media player, a custom image editor, and a networked chat application. These projects will challenge you to apply your Qt skills in practical scenarios and solidify your understanding of the framework.
- **Part V: Best Practices and Beyond:** The final part focuses on industry best practices, coding standards, design patterns, and troubleshooting techniques. We also provide guidance on building your Qt developer career, including tips on creating a portfolio, preparing for interviews, and navigating the job market.

Online Resources and Community Support

To complement your learning experience, we provide a wealth of online resources, including code repositories, downloadable project files, and video tutorials. We encourage you to visit our website [insert website URL] to access these materials and connect with a vibrant community of Qt developers. Feel free to ask questions, share your projects, and collaborate with fellow learners.

Embark on Your Qt Journey

With its cross-platform capabilities, extensive feature set, and supportive community, Qt empowers you to create exceptional GUI applications that leave a lasting impression. As you embark on this exciting journey, remember that the key to mastery lies in practice, experimentation, and a genuine passion for crafting user experiences that delight and inspire.

Part I: Getting Started with Qt 6

Chapter 1: Installing and Setting Up Qt 6

Downloading and Installing Qt 6

Embarking on your Qt journey begins with acquiring and installing the necessary tools. Thankfully, the process is straightforward and well-documented. In this section, we'll guide you through the steps involved in downloading and installing Qt 6, ensuring a smooth and successful setup.

1. Acquiring the Qt Installer

The first step is to obtain the Qt installer, which serves as the gateway to the Qt development ecosystem. Head over to the official Qt website (https://www.qt.io/download) and navigate to the download section. Here, you'll find various options tailored to different operating systems and use cases.

2. Selecting the Appropriate Qt Version

Qt offers two primary editions: the open-source edition and the commercial edition. The open-source edition is ideal for most developers, providing access to a wealth of features and capabilities under the GPLv3 or LGPLv3 licenses. The commercial edition offers additional benefits, such as dedicated support and access to proprietary tools, making it suitable for enterprise-level development.

For the purposes of this book, we'll focus on the open-source edition, which is more than sufficient for learning and building impressive GUI applications. Within the open-source edition, you'll have the choice between the online installer and the offline installer. The online installer is typically smaller in size and downloads the necessary components during the installation process. The offline installer, on the other hand, contains all the required files, making it a suitable option if you have limited internet connectivity or prefer a self-contained installation.

3. Initiating the Installation Process

Once you've downloaded the Qt installer, locate the executable file on your system and launch it. The installer will guide you through a series of steps, allowing you to customize the installation according to your preferences.

4. Customizing the Installation

During the installation process, you'll be presented with various options to tailor Qt to your specific needs. Pay close attention to the following:

- **Qt Components:** Qt comprises numerous components, each catering to different functionalities. Select the components that align with your development goals. For GUI development, ensure you include the following essential components:
    - **Qt Core:** The foundation of Qt, providing core non-GUI classes and functionalities.
    - **Qt GUI:** The core GUI module, offering widgets, layouts, and other GUI elements.
    - **Qt Widgets:** A comprehensive collection of pre-built GUI widgets.
    - **Qt QML:** The declarative language for designing fluid and dynamic UIs.
    - **Qt Quick:** The module for building QML-based applications.
    - **Qt Creator:** The integrated development environment (IDE) tailored for Qt development.
- **Installation Path:** Choose a suitable location on your system to install Qt. Avoid

spaces or special characters in the path to prevent potential issues.
- **Start Menu Shortcuts:** Decide whether you want to create shortcuts in your system's start menu for easy access to Qt Creator and other Qt tools.

5. Completing the Installation

Once you've made your selections, proceed with the installation. The installer will download and install the chosen Qt components, which may take some time depending on your internet connection and the number of selected components.

6. Launching Qt Creator

After the installation is complete, you can launch Qt Creator, the powerful IDE that streamlines Qt development. Qt Creator provides a user-friendly interface, code editor, visual design tools, and debugging capabilities, making it an indispensable companion for your Qt projects.

Troubleshooting Tips

While the installation process is generally smooth, you might encounter occasional hiccups. Here are some common issues and their solutions:

- **Installer Errors:** If you encounter errors during the installation, ensure you have a stable internet connection and sufficient disk space. You can also try re-downloading the installer or running it as an administrator.
- **Missing Components:** If you realize you missed selecting essential components during the installation, you can always relaunch the installer and modify your selections.
- **Path Issues:** If Qt Creator or other Qt tools fail to launch, double-check the installation path and ensure it doesn't contain spaces or special characters.

With Qt 6 successfully installed on your system, you're now equipped to embark on your GUI development journey. In the upcoming chapters, we'll delve deeper into Qt's core concepts, empowering you to craft stunning and interactive user interfaces that elevate your C++ applications to new heights.

Choosing the Right Qt Components

As you embark on your Qt installation journey, a crucial decision awaits: selecting the appropriate Qt components that align with your development goals. Qt's modular architecture offers a vast array of components, each catering to specific functionalities and use cases. While the abundance of choices empowers you to tailor Qt to your precise needs, it can also be overwhelming for newcomers. In this section, we'll guide you through the essential Qt components required for GUI development, ensuring you have the necessary tools at your disposal.

Essential Qt Components for GUI Development

1. **Qt Core:** The bedrock of the Qt framework, Qt Core provides essential non-GUI classes and functionalities that underpin the entire Qt ecosystem. It encompasses fundamental data types, containers, algorithms, input/output operations, and more. Qt Core is a mandatory component for any Qt project, serving as the foundation upon which other modules are built.
2. **Qt GUI:** The core GUI module, Qt GUI, forms the backbone of Qt's graphical user interface capabilities. It offers a comprehensive set of classes for creating and managing windows, widgets, layouts, events, and other GUI elements. Qt GUI is indispensable for building any Qt-based graphical application.

3. **Qt Widgets:** A treasure trove of pre-built GUI widgets, Qt Widgets provides a rich collection of ready-to-use components for constructing user interfaces. From buttons and labels to tables and tree views, Qt Widgets offers a wide range of visual elements that accelerate development and streamline the creation of interactive interfaces.
4. **Qt QML:** Qt QML introduces a declarative language for designing fluid and dynamic user interfaces. With its JavaScript-like syntax and intuitive structure, QML empowers you to describe the visual appearance and behavior of your UI in a concise and expressive manner. QML's seamless integration with C++ allows you to leverage the power of both worlds, combining the performance of C++ with the flexibility of QML.
5. **Qt Quick:** The module responsible for building QML-based applications, Qt Quick provides the runtime environment and infrastructure for executing QML code. It seamlessly integrates with Qt GUI, enabling you to combine traditional widgets with QML elements to create hybrid UIs that leverage the strengths of both approaches.

6. **Qt Creator:** The integrated development environment (IDE) purpose-built for Qt development, Qt Creator streamlines the entire development workflow. It offers a user-friendly interface, code editor with syntax highlighting and auto-completion, visual design tools for crafting UIs, debugging capabilities, and seamless integration with Qt's build system. Qt Creator significantly enhances productivity and facilitates efficient Qt development.

Additional Considerations

While the aforementioned components form the core foundation for Qt GUI development, you may consider including additional modules based on your specific project requirements. For example, if your application involves database interactions, you'll need to include the Qt SQL module. Similarly, if your application requires network communication, the Qt Network module becomes essential.

Carefully evaluate the functionalities you need and select the corresponding Qt components accordingly. Remember, you can always modify your selections later if your project requirements evolve.

Choosing the right Qt components is a crucial step in setting up your Qt development environment. By selecting the essential modules outlined in this section, you'll equip yourself with the necessary tools to build impressive GUI applications with Qt. As you progress through this book, you'll gain a deeper understanding of these components and their interplay, empowering you to craft user interfaces that are both visually appealing and functionally rich.

Configuring Qt Creator

Once you've successfully installed Qt 6 and selected the appropriate components, it's time to configure Qt Creator, your gateway to a streamlined and efficient development experience. Qt Creator offers a plethora of settings and customizations to personalize your workflow and optimize your productivity. In this section, we'll guide you through the essential configurations that lay the foundation for a seamless Qt development journey.

1. Setting Up Kits

Kits in Qt Creator represent combinations of compilers, debuggers, and Qt versions that define the build and run environment for your projects. To ensure your projects compile and run correctly, it's crucial to configure kits that align with your installed Qt version and target platforms.

- Navigate to `Tools > Options > Kits` in Qt Creator.
- In the `Kits` tab, you'll find a list of detected kits. If you've installed Qt 6 correctly, you should see a kit corresponding to your Qt version and compiler.
- Verify that the kit's details, such as the Qt version, compiler, and debugger, match your setup.
- If necessary, create new kits or modify existing ones to match your specific requirements.

2. Customizing the Editor

Qt Creator's code editor is a powerful tool that enhances your coding experience with features like syntax highlighting, code completion, and code navigation. Customize the editor settings to suit your preferences and coding style.

- Navigate to `Tools > Options > Text Editor` in Qt Creator.
- In the `Behavior` tab, adjust settings such as tab size, indentation, and auto-completion behavior.

- Explore the `Fonts & Colors` tab to personalize the editor's appearance with your preferred font, colors, and themes.
- Experiment with other editor settings to fine-tune your coding environment.

3. Configuring Build and Run Settings

Qt Creator streamlines the build and run process for your projects, allowing you to compile, execute, and debug your applications with ease. Configure the build and run settings to ensure seamless execution and efficient debugging.

- Navigate to `Projects > Build & Run` in Qt Creator.
- In the `Build Settings` tab, verify that the build directory and shadow build options are set according to your preferences.
- In the `Run Settings` tab, configure the command-line arguments and working directory for your application.
- Explore the `Debugger Settings` tab to customize the debugger behavior and set breakpoints for efficient debugging.

4. Managing Plugins

Qt Creator's functionality can be extended through plugins, which provide additional features and integrations. Manage your plugins to tailor Qt Creator to your specific needs.

- Navigate to `Help > About Plugins` in Qt Creator.
- In the `Plugins` dialog, enable or disable plugins as needed.
- Explore the available plugins and install additional ones from the Qt Marketplace if required.

5. Personalizing the Interface

Qt Creator's interface is highly customizable, allowing you to arrange tool windows, menus, and toolbars to suit your workflow. Personalize the interface to create a comfortable and productive development environment.

- Experiment with different window layouts by dragging and dropping tool windows.
- Customize menus and toolbars by right-clicking on them and selecting `Customize`.
- Explore the `Environment` settings in `Tools > Options` to further personalize Qt Creator's behavior.

Configuring Qt Creator to align with your preferences and project requirements is a crucial step in maximizing your productivity and efficiency as a Qt developer. By setting up kits, customizing the editor, configuring build and run settings, managing plugins, and personalizing the interface, you can create a development environment that fosters creativity and streamlines your workflow.

Creating Your First Qt Project

With Qt 6 installed and Qt Creator configured to your liking, it's time to embark on the exciting journey of creating your first Qt project. This initial endeavor will introduce you to the fundamental workflow of Qt development, laying the groundwork for more complex and sophisticated projects in the future. Let's dive in and bring your first Qt GUI application to life.

1. Launching Qt Creator

Locate the Qt Creator icon on your desktop or in your system's start menu and launch the application. You'll be greeted with Qt Creator's welcome screen, offering various options to get started.

2. Creating a New Project

To create a new Qt project, click on the "New Project" button or navigate to `File > New File or Project`. Qt Creator will present you with a dialog box showcasing a variety of project templates, each catering to different types of applications.

3. Selecting the Project Template

For our first project, let's choose the "Qt Widgets Application" template. This template provides a basic structure for building GUI applications using Qt Widgets, the traditional approach to Qt GUI development.

4. Configuring Project Details

After selecting the template, you'll be prompted to provide some essential details about your project:

- **Project Name:** Choose a descriptive name for your project, such as "MyFirstQtApp".
- **Project Location:** Select a suitable directory on your system to store your project files.
- **Build System:** Qt Creator supports various build systems, including qmake and CMake. For simplicity, let's stick with qmake for this initial project.

- **Kit Selection:** Ensure the correct kit is selected for your project. The kit should correspond to your installed Qt version and target platform.

5. Designing the User Interface

Once you've configured the project details, Qt Creator will generate the basic project structure and open the main window's design view. The design view allows you to visually arrange widgets and construct your user interface.

- From the widget box on the left, drag and drop a "PushButton" widget onto the main window.
- Double-click on the push button and change its text to "Hello, Qt!".
- Resize and reposition the push button as desired.

6. Connecting Signals and Slots

Qt's signal-slot mechanism enables communication between objects in your application. Let's connect the push button's "clicked" signal to a slot that will display a message when the button is pressed.

- Right-click on the push button and select "Go to slot...".

- In the dialog box, choose the "clicked()" signal and click "OK".
- Qt Creator will generate a slot function in your main window's header and source files.
- Inside the slot function, add the following code:

C++

```
QMessageBox::information(this,    "Qt Greeting", "Hello from Qt!");
```

7. Building and Running the Application

With the user interface designed and the signal-slot connection established, it's time to build and run your application.

- Click on the green "Run" button in Qt Creator's toolbar or press `Ctrl+R`.
- Qt Creator will compile your code and launch the application.
- You should see a window with a push button labeled "Hello, Qt!".

- Click on the button, and a message box will appear, displaying the greeting "Hello from Qt!".

Congratulations!

You've successfully created your first Qt GUI application. While this project is simple, it demonstrates the fundamental workflow of Qt development and serves as a stepping stone for more ambitious endeavors.

Chapter 2: Essential C++ Concepts for Qt

Object-Oriented Programming in C++

Qt is deeply rooted in the principles of object-oriented programming (OOP), a paradigm that revolves around the concept of objects, which encapsulate data and behavior. Understanding OOP is crucial for effectively leveraging Qt's capabilities and building well-structured and maintainable GUI applications. In this section, we'll delve into the core tenets of OOP in C++, providing a solid foundation for your Qt development journey.

Classes and Objects: The Building Blocks

At the heart of OOP lies the concept of classes and objects. A class serves as a blueprint or template for creating objects, defining their properties (data) and methods (behavior). An object, on the other hand, is an instance of a class, representing a concrete entity in your program.

Let's consider a simple example:

C++

```
class Car {
```

```cpp
public:
    // Properties
    std::string color;
    int numDoors;

    // Methods
    void startEngine() {
        std::cout << "Engine started!" << std::endl;
    }

    void openDoor(int doorNumber) {
        std::cout << "Opening door " << doorNumber << std::endl;
    }
};

int main() {
    Car myCar;
    myCar.color = "red";
    myCar.numDoors = 4;

    myCar.startEngine();
    myCar.openDoor(2);

    return 0;
}
```

In this example, we define a `Car` class with properties `color` and `numDoors`, and methods `startEngine()` and `openDoor()`. In the `main()` function, we create an object `myCar` of the `Car` class, set its properties, and invoke its methods.

Inheritance: Extending Functionality

Inheritance is a powerful OOP concept that allows you to create new classes (derived classes) based on existing classes (base classes). The derived class inherits the properties and methods of the base class, enabling code reuse and promoting a hierarchical organization of classes.

Let's extend our `Car` example:

C++

```
class ElectricCar : public Car {
public:
    void chargeBattery() {
             std::cout << "Battery charging..." << std::endl;
    }
};
```

```
int main() {
    ElectricCar myElectricCar;
    myElectricCar.color = "blue";
    myElectricCar.numDoors = 2;

    myElectricCar.startEngine();   // Inherited from Car
    myElectricCar.openDoor(1);     // Inherited from Car
    myElectricCar.chargeBattery();

    return 0;
}
```

Here, we create an `ElectricCar` class that inherits from the `Car` class. The `ElectricCar` class inherits the properties and methods of `Car` and adds its own method `chargeBattery()`.

Polymorphism: Flexibility and Adaptability

Polymorphism allows objects of different classes to be treated as objects of a common base class. This enables you to write code that can operate on a variety of objects, promoting flexibility and adaptability in your applications.

Let's illustrate polymorphism:

C++

```cpp
class Vehicle {
public:
    virtual void start() = 0; // Pure virtual function
};

class Car : public Vehicle {
public:
    void start() override {
        std::cout << "Car engine started!" << std::endl;
    }
};

class ElectricCar : public Vehicle {
public:
    void start() override {
        std::cout << "Electric car powered on!" << std::endl;
    }
};
```

```
int main() {
    Vehicle* myVehicle;

    myVehicle = new Car();
    myVehicle->start(); // Output: Car engine started!

    delete myVehicle;
    myVehicle = new ElectricCar();
    myVehicle->start(); // Output: Electric car powered on!

    delete myVehicle;
    return 0;
}
```

In this example, we define a `Vehicle` base class with a pure virtual function `start()`. The `Car` and `ElectricCar` classes inherit from `Vehicle` and provide their own implementations of the `start()` function. In the `main()` function, we create pointers to `Vehicle` objects and assign them to `Car` and `ElectricCar` objects. When we call the `start()` function through the `Vehicle` pointers, the appropriate implementation is executed based on the actual object type, showcasing the power of polymorphism.

Encapsulation: Data Protection and Abstraction

Encapsulation involves bundling data and the methods that operate on that data within a single unit, the class. This protects the data from unauthorized access and modification, promoting data integrity and abstraction.

In our `Car` example, the `color` and `numDoors` properties are encapsulated within the `Car` class. Access to these properties is controlled through the class's methods, ensuring that they are used and modified in a consistent and predictable manner.

Object-oriented programming provides a structured and organized approach to software development, enabling you to build complex applications with clarity and maintainability. By understanding the core OOP concepts of classes, objects, inheritance, polymorphism, and encapsulation, you'll be well-equipped to harness Qt's power and create GUI applications that are both robust and elegant.

Classes, Objects, and Inheritance

In the realm of Qt, the concepts of classes, objects, and inheritance form the bedrock of GUI development. These object-oriented programming (OOP) principles empower you to structure your code, create reusable components, and build complex user interfaces with clarity and maintainability. In this section, we'll explore these concepts in the context of Qt, showcasing their practical application and significance in crafting robust GUI applications.

Classes: Blueprints for Objects

In Qt, as in C++, a class serves as a blueprint for creating objects. It defines the properties (data) and methods (behavior) that an object of that class will possess. Think of a class as a template that outlines the structure and capabilities of its corresponding objects.

For instance, let's consider the `QPushButton` class, a fundamental building block in Qt GUI development. The `QPushButton` class encapsulates the properties and methods necessary to create and manage push buttons in your application. It defines properties like the button's text, size, and icon, as well as methods for handling user interactions, such as clicks and releases.

Objects: Instances of Classes

An object is a concrete instance of a class, representing a specific entity in your program. When you create an object of a class, you allocate memory to store its properties and gain access to its methods.

Continuing with our `QPushButton` example, you can create multiple push button objects, each with its own unique set of properties and behavior. One button might display the text "OK," while another might show an icon representing a save operation. Each button object is an independent entity, capable of responding to user interactions and triggering specific actions within your application.

Inheritance: Extending Functionality

Inheritance is a powerful mechanism in OOP that enables you to create new classes (derived classes) based on existing classes (base classes). The derived class inherits the properties and methods of the base class, allowing you to reuse code and extend functionality without reinventing the wheel.

In Qt, inheritance plays a crucial role in customizing and enhancing the behavior of existing widgets. For example, you might create a custom button class that inherits from `QPushButton` and adds additional features like a progress indicator or a custom context menu. By leveraging inheritance, you can build upon the foundation provided by Qt's built-in classes and tailor them to your specific needs.

Let's illustrate the concept of inheritance with a code example:

C++

```
class MyCustomButton : public QPushButton {
    Q_OBJECT // Necessary for signals and slots

public:
    explicit MyCustomButton(QWidget *parent = nullptr);

signals:
    void customButtonClicked();

public slots:
    void handleCustomButtonClick();
```

```
private:
    // Additional properties and
methods specific to MyCustomButton
};
```

In this example, we define a new class called `MyCustomButton` that inherits from `QPushButton`. This new class inherits all the properties and methods of `QPushButton`, allowing us to create custom buttons that behave like standard push buttons but with additional functionalities. We've also added a custom signal `customButtonClicked()` and a corresponding slot `handleCustomButtonClick()` to handle specific actions triggered by our custom button.

The Power of Inheritance in Qt

Inheritance permeates the entire Qt framework, providing a flexible and extensible architecture for building GUI applications. Qt's core classes, such as `QWidget`, `QObject`, and `QLayout`, serve as base classes for countless other classes, enabling you to create a vast hierarchy of interconnected objects that form the backbone of your application.

By understanding and leveraging inheritance, you can:

- **Reuse code:** Inherit functionality from existing classes, eliminating the need to rewrite common code.
- **Customize behavior:** Extend and modify the behavior of base classes to suit your specific requirements.
- **Organize code:** Create a hierarchical structure of classes, promoting clarity and maintainability.
- **Facilitate polymorphism:** Treat objects of different classes as objects of a common base class, enabling flexible and adaptable code.

Classes, objects, and inheritance are fundamental OOP concepts that play a pivotal role in Qt GUI development. By mastering these principles, you'll gain the ability to structure your code effectively, create reusable components, and build complex user interfaces with ease.

Memory Management with Smart Pointers

In the realm of C++ programming, memory management is a critical aspect that demands careful attention. Traditional C++ relied on manual memory allocation and deallocation using `new` and `delete`, which, while powerful, could lead to memory leaks and dangling pointers if not handled meticulously. Qt, however, embraces modern C++ practices and encourages the use of smart pointers, intelligent objects that automate memory management, significantly reducing the risk of errors and enhancing code safety. In this section, we'll explore the concept of smart pointers and their indispensable role in Qt development.

The Perils of Manual Memory Management

Before diving into the world of smart pointers, let's briefly revisit the challenges associated with manual memory management in C++. When you allocate memory dynamically using `new`, you assume the responsibility of explicitly deallocating it using `delete` when it's no longer needed. Failure to do so results in memory leaks, where allocated memory remains inaccessible, gradually consuming system resources and potentially leading to application crashes.

Furthermore, dangling pointers can arise when you delete memory prematurely, leaving pointers pointing to invalid memory locations. Accessing such pointers can trigger undefined behavior and wreak havoc on your application's stability.

Smart Pointers to the Rescue

Smart pointers offer a safer and more convenient approach to memory management in C++. They act as wrappers around raw pointers, automatically managing the lifetime of the allocated memory. When a smart pointer goes out of scope or is reassigned, it automatically deallocates the associated memory, eliminating the need for manual `delete` calls and significantly reducing the risk of memory leaks.

Types of Smart Pointers

C++11 introduced three primary types of smart pointers:

1. `unique_ptr`: Represents exclusive ownership of the managed object. Only one `unique_ptr` can point to a given object at any time. When a `unique_ptr` goes out of scope, it automatically deletes the owned object.

2. `shared_ptr`: Enables shared ownership of the managed object. Multiple `shared_ptr` objects can point to the same object, and the object is deleted only when the last `shared_ptr` pointing to it is destroyed.
3. `weak_ptr`: Provides a non-owning reference to an object managed by a `shared_ptr`. `weak_ptr` objects don't contribute to the object's reference count and can be used to observe an object without affecting its lifetime.

Smart Pointers in Qt

Qt seamlessly integrates with smart pointers, encouraging their use throughout the framework. Many Qt classes, especially those involved in resource management, leverage smart pointers internally to ensure proper memory handling.

For example, the `QImage` class, used for representing images in Qt, employs a `shared_ptr` internally to manage the image data. This ensures that the image data remains valid as long as any `QImage` object references it, preventing premature deallocation and potential crashes.

Best Practices

When working with Qt, adhere to the following best practices regarding smart pointers:

- **Prefer smart pointers over raw pointers:** Whenever possible, use smart pointers to manage dynamically allocated memory. This minimizes the risk of memory leaks and dangling pointers.
- **Choose the appropriate smart pointer type:** Use `unique_ptr` for exclusive ownership, `shared_ptr` for shared ownership, and `weak_ptr` for non-owning references.
- **Avoid manual `new` and `delete`:** Rely on smart pointers to handle memory allocation and deallocation automatically.
- **Be mindful of ownership transfer:** When passing smart pointers between functions or objects, carefully consider ownership semantics to prevent unintended behavior.

Example

Let's illustrate the use of smart pointers in a Qt context:

C++

```
#include <QImage>
```

```cpp
#include <memory>

int main() {
    std::shared_ptr<QImage> image = std::make_shared<QImage>("image.jpg");

    // Use the image...

    return 0;
}
```

In this example, we create a `shared_ptr` to manage a `QImage` object. The `image` smart pointer ensures that the image data remains valid throughout its lifetime, even if we pass it to other functions or objects. When the `image` smart pointer goes out of scope, the associated `QImage` object and its underlying data are automatically deallocated.

Smart pointers are an indispensable tool in modern C++ development, and Qt wholeheartedly embraces their use. By automating memory management, smart pointers enhance code safety, reduce the risk of errors, and promote cleaner and more maintainable code.

Lambda Expressions and the Standard Library

Modern C++ has evolved to become a more expressive and powerful language, thanks in part to the introduction of lambda expressions and the expansion of the standard library. These features offer concise syntax, enhanced functionality, and improved code readability, making them valuable tools in Qt development. In this section, we'll explore lambda expressions and the standard library, showcasing their practical applications and benefits in the context of GUI programming.

Lambda Expressions: Anonymous Functions

Lambda expressions, introduced in C++11, provide a way to define anonymous functions, also known as closures. These compact functions can be created and used inline, often eliminating the need for separate named functions and promoting code clarity.

The basic syntax of a lambda expression is as follows:

C++

```
[capture list] (parameter list) ->
return type {
    // Function body
}
```

Let's break down the components:

- **Capture list:** Specifies variables from the surrounding scope that the lambda expression can access.
- **Parameter list:** Declares the parameters that the lambda expression accepts.
- **Return type:** Indicates the type of value that the lambda expression returns. This can be omitted if the return type can be deduced automatically.
- **Function body:** Contains the code that the lambda expression executes.

Lambda Expressions in Qt

Lambda expressions find numerous applications in Qt, particularly when working with signals and slots, event handling, and asynchronous operations. Their concise syntax and ability to capture variables from the surrounding scope make them ideal for handling callbacks and event-driven programming.

Let's illustrate the use of lambda expressions in a Qt context:

C++

```
QPushButton* button = new QPushButton("Click me!", this);
connect(button, &QPushButton::clicked, [this]() {
    QMessageBox::information(this, "Button Clicked", "You clicked the button!");
});
```

In this example, we create a `QPushButton` and connect its `clicked` signal to a lambda expression. When the button is clicked, the lambda expression is executed, displaying a message box. The lambda expression captures the `this` pointer, allowing it to access the parent widget and display the message box correctly.

The Standard Library: A Treasure Trove of Functionality

The C++ standard library is a vast collection of classes, functions, and algorithms that provide essential functionality for various programming tasks. From containers and algorithms to input/output operations and string manipulation, the standard library offers a wealth of tools to streamline development and enhance code efficiency.

In Qt development, the standard library complements Qt's own classes and functions, providing additional capabilities and flexibility. For example, you might use standard library containers like `std::vector` or `std::map` to store and manage data within your Qt application. You might also leverage standard library algorithms like `std::sort` or `std::find` to process and manipulate data efficiently.

Best Practices

When working with lambda expressions and the standard library in Qt, consider the following best practices:

- **Use lambda expressions judiciously:** While lambda expressions offer convenience, avoid overuse, especially for complex logic that might benefit from a separate named function.
- **Capture variables carefully:** Be mindful of capturing variables by value or by reference in lambda expressions to avoid unintended side effects or dangling references.
- **Leverage the standard library:** Explore the standard library's rich functionality to streamline your code and enhance its efficiency.
- **Familiarize yourself with Qt's algorithms and containers:** Qt provides its own set of algorithms and containers that are optimized for Qt development. Consider using them when appropriate.

Lambda expressions and the standard library are powerful features of modern C++ that can significantly enhance your Qt development experience. By embracing these tools, you can write more concise, expressive, and maintainable code, ultimately leading to more robust and efficient GUI applications.

Error Handling and Exception Handling

In the realm of software development, errors are an inevitable reality. Whether it's invalid user input, unexpected network failures, or resource constraints, your Qt applications must be equipped to handle errors gracefully and prevent catastrophic crashes. C++ offers two primary mechanisms for dealing with errors: error handling and exception handling. In this section, we'll explore these mechanisms in the context of Qt, equipping you with the knowledge to build robust and resilient GUI applications.

Error Handling: The Traditional Approach

Error handling in C++ traditionally involves returning error codes or setting error flags to indicate the success or failure of an operation. This approach requires careful checking of return values or error states after each function call, ensuring that errors are detected and handled appropriately.

Let's illustrate traditional error handling in a Qt context:

C++

```
QFile file("data.txt");
```

```
if   (!file.open(QIODevice::ReadOnly |
QIODevice::Text)) {
        QMessageBox::critical(nullptr,
"Error", "Could not open file!");
    return;
}

QTextStream in(&file);
while (!in.atEnd()) {
    QString line = in.readLine();
    // Process the line...
}
```

In this example, we attempt to open a file using `QFile`. We check the return value of the `open()` function to ensure the file was opened successfully. If an error occurs, we display an error message and exit the program.

Exception Handling: A Structured Approach

Exception handling provides a more structured and centralized approach to error management in C++. It involves throwing exceptions to signal errors and catching them in designated blocks of code to handle the exceptional situations.

Let's rewrite the previous example using exception handling:

C++

```
try {
    QFile file("data.txt");
        file.open(QIODevice::ReadOnly | QIODevice::Text);

    QTextStream in(&file);
    while (!in.atEnd()) {
        QString line = in.readLine();
        // Process the line...
    }
} catch (const std::exception& e) {
        QMessageBox::critical(nullptr, "Error", e.what());
}
```

In this version, we enclose the file operations within a `try` block. If an exception is thrown during file opening or reading, the `catch` block is executed, displaying an error message to the user.

Choosing the Right Approach

Both error handling and exception handling have their merits and drawbacks. Error handling offers fine-grained control and can be more efficient in certain scenarios, while exception handling provides a structured and centralized way to manage errors, promoting code clarity and maintainability.

In Qt, the choice between error handling and exception handling often depends on the specific Qt classes and functions you're working with. Some Qt functions return error codes or set error flags, while others throw exceptions to signal errors. It's crucial to consult the Qt documentation for each class or function to understand its error handling mechanism.

Best Practices

Regardless of the chosen approach, adhere to the following best practices for error management in Qt:

- **Handle errors gracefully:** Always anticipate and handle potential errors to prevent

crashes and provide informative feedback to the user.
- **Use descriptive error messages:** Craft clear and concise error messages that guide the user in resolving the issue.
- **Log errors:** Consider logging errors to a file or console for debugging and troubleshooting purposes.
- **Test thoroughly:** Rigorously test your application under various conditions to uncover and address potential errors.

Error handling and exception handling are essential tools for building robust and resilient Qt applications. By understanding these mechanisms and employing best practices, you can ensure that your applications gracefully handle errors, providing a seamless and user-friendly experience even in the face of unexpected situations. As you progress through this book, you'll encounter various scenarios where error management plays a crucial role. Embrace these techniques, and let them fortify your Qt applications against the inevitable challenges of the real world.

Chapter 3: Building Your First Qt GUI Application

Understanding Qt Widgets

In the realm of Qt GUI development, widgets reign supreme as the fundamental building blocks of your user interfaces. These versatile components encapsulate visual elements, interactive features, and layout capabilities, empowering you to craft intuitive and engaging interfaces that seamlessly connect with your users. In this section, we'll embark on a journey to explore the world of Qt widgets, unraveling their essence, versatility, and pivotal role in shaping your GUI applications.

The Essence of Qt Widgets

At its core, a Qt widget is a self-contained graphical user interface element that resides within a window. It can be as simple as a button or a label, or as complex as a table or a tree view. Widgets provide visual representation, respond to user interactions, and often encapsulate underlying data and logic.

Qt boasts an extensive library of pre-built widgets, catering to a wide range of functionalities and use cases. These widgets encompass buttons, labels, text edits, combo boxes, checkboxes, radio buttons, sliders, progress bars, tables, tree views, and much more. This rich collection of components empowers you to assemble intricate and feature-rich user interfaces without reinventing the wheel.

The Versatility of Qt Widgets

Qt widgets are inherently versatile, allowing you to customize their appearance, behavior, and layout to align with your design vision. You can modify their properties, such as size, position, text, and color, to achieve the desired visual aesthetic. Furthermore, you can connect signals and slots to widgets, enabling them to communicate with other objects in your application and respond to user interactions in a dynamic and interactive manner.

Qt's layout system further enhances the versatility of widgets, enabling you to arrange them in a structured and organized manner within your windows. Layouts automatically adjust the size and position of widgets based on the window's dimensions and the relationships between widgets, ensuring a visually pleasing and responsive interface across different screen sizes and resolutions.

Qt Widgets in Action

Let's take a closer look at some commonly used Qt widgets and their applications:

- **QPushButton:** The quintessential button widget, `QPushButton` enables users to trigger actions within your application. You can customize its text, icon, and appearance to create visually appealing and informative buttons.
- **QLabel:** The label widget, `QLabel`, displays text or images within your GUI. It's ideal for providing instructions, displaying status messages, or showcasing visual content.
- **QLineEdit:** The line edit widget, `QLineEdit`, allows users to input and edit text. It supports features like password masking, input validation, and auto-completion, making it suitable for various data entry scenarios.
- **QComboBox:** The combo box widget, `QComboBox`, presents a dropdown list of options for users to select from. It's a space-efficient alternative to radio buttons or checkboxes when you have multiple choices.
- **QCheckBox:** The checkbox widget, `QCheckBox`, allows users to toggle options on or off. It's commonly used for settings or

preferences where multiple selections are possible.
- **QRadioButton:** The radio button widget, `QRadioButton`, presents a group of mutually exclusive options. Users can select only one option from the group at a time.
- **QSlider:** The slider widget, `QSlider`, enables users to select a value within a specified range by moving a handle along a track. It's useful for adjusting volume, brightness, or other continuous values.
- **QProgressBar:** The progress bar widget, `QProgressBar`, visually represents the progress of a task or operation. It's ideal for providing feedback to users during lengthy processes.
- **QTableWidget:** The table widget, `QTableWidget`, displays data in a tabular format with rows and columns. It supports sorting, filtering, and editing, making it suitable for presenting structured information.
- **QTreeWidget:** The tree widget, `QTreeWidget`, displays hierarchical data in a tree-like structure. It allows users to expand and collapse branches to navigate and explore the data hierarchy.

These are just a few examples of the vast array of Qt widgets at your disposal. As you delve deeper into Qt development, you'll encounter many more widgets, each with its own unique capabilities and applications.

Qt widgets are the cornerstone of GUI development in Qt, providing the visual elements, interactive features, and layout capabilities necessary to build compelling user interfaces. By understanding the essence and versatility of Qt widgets, you'll be empowered to craft applications that are not only functional but also aesthetically pleasing and user-friendly.

Designing the User Interface with Qt Designer

Qt Designer emerges as an invaluable ally in the quest to craft visually appealing and user-friendly interfaces. This intuitive visual design tool empowers you to arrange widgets, customize their properties, and preview your creations in real-time, all without writing a single line of code. In this section, we'll embark on a guided tour of Qt Designer, unraveling its features and demonstrating its prowess in streamlining the UI design process.

Entering the Design Realm

Within Qt Creator, double-click on the `mainwindow.ui` file in your project's file tree. This action launches Qt Designer, unveiling a canvas where your creative vision will take shape. The canvas represents the main window of your application, providing a blank slate for you to populate with widgets and arrange them into a cohesive interface.

Widget Wonderland

On the left side of Qt Designer, you'll find the "Widget Box," a treasure trove of pre-built Qt widgets. These widgets span a wide spectrum of functionalities, encompassing buttons, labels, text edits, combo boxes, checkboxes, radio buttons, sliders, progress bars, tables, tree views, and much more. Each widget is represented by an icon and a descriptive label, making it easy to identify and select the desired component.

Drag, Drop, and Arrange

Designing your UI in Qt Designer is as simple as dragging widgets from the Widget Box and dropping them onto the canvas. Once placed, you can resize, reposition, and align widgets using intuitive drag-and-drop gestures and alignment tools. Qt Designer's grid and snapping features further facilitate precise positioning and arrangement, ensuring a visually harmonious interface.

Property Playground

Every widget in Qt possesses a set of properties that define its appearance, behavior, and functionality. Qt Designer provides a convenient "Property Editor" on the right side, allowing you to modify these properties with ease. You can change a button's text, adjust a label's font, set a slider's range, or configure a table's column headers, all within the Property Editor's intuitive interface.

Layout Mastery

Arranging widgets haphazardly on the canvas would result in a chaotic and unappealing interface. Qt's layout system comes to the rescue, enabling you to organize widgets in a structured and responsive manner. Qt Designer offers several layout managers, including horizontal layouts, vertical layouts, grid layouts, and form layouts. These layouts automatically adjust the size and position of widgets based on the window's dimensions and the relationships between widgets, ensuring a visually pleasing and adaptable interface across different screen sizes and resolutions.

Previewing Your Creation

As you design your UI, Qt Designer provides a real-time preview, allowing you to visualize your creation as it would appear in the final application. This instant feedback loop empowers you to iterate on your design, experiment with different widget arrangements and property settings, and fine-tune the visual aesthetic until you achieve the desired look and feel.

Seamless Integration with Code

Qt Designer seamlessly integrates with your C++ code, generating UI files that can be easily incorporated into your project. These UI files define the structure and properties of your interface, freeing you from the burden of manually constructing widgets and layouts in code. Qt's signal-slot mechanism further bridges the gap between design and functionality, enabling you to connect signals emitted by widgets to slots in your C++ code, thereby defining the behavior and interactivity of your application.

Qt Designer is a powerful and intuitive visual design tool that streamlines the UI design process, empowering you to craft visually appealing and user-friendly interfaces with ease. By leveraging its drag-and-drop functionality, property editor, layout managers, and real-time preview, you can iterate on your designs, experiment with different approaches, and achieve the perfect balance of aesthetics and functionality.

Laying Out Widgets with Layouts

In the realm of GUI design, achieving a visually pleasing and responsive interface requires more than just placing widgets on a canvas. It demands a structured and organized approach to arranging these widgets, ensuring they adapt gracefully to different window sizes and screen resolutions. Qt's layout system provides the answer, empowering you to create dynamic and adaptable interfaces that maintain their aesthetic appeal and usability across various platforms and devices. In this section, we'll delve into the intricacies of Qt layouts, exploring their types, properties, and application in crafting well-structured and visually harmonious GUIs.

The Power of Layouts

At its core, a layout in Qt is a specialized container that manages the size and position of its child widgets. It acts as an invisible guiding force, orchestrating the arrangement of widgets within a window or another container widget. Layouts automatically adjust the size and position of their child widgets based on the available space, ensuring a visually pleasing and responsive interface even when the window is resized or the screen resolution changes.

Qt offers several types of layouts, each with its own unique characteristics and use cases:

1. **QHBoxLayout:** Arranges widgets horizontally in a single row.
2. **QVBoxLayout:** Arranges widgets vertically in a single column.
3. **QGridLayout:** Arranges widgets in a grid-like structure with rows and columns.
4. **QFormLayout:** Arranges widgets in a two-column layout, typically used for forms or data entry interfaces.

Applying Layouts in Qt Designer

Qt Designer seamlessly integrates with Qt's layout system, providing a visual and intuitive way to apply layouts to your widgets. To apply a layout, select the desired widgets on the canvas, right-click, and choose "Lay Out" from the context menu. Qt Designer will then apply the selected layout to the chosen widgets, automatically adjusting their size and position accordingly.

Fine-Tuning Layouts

Once a layout is applied, you can further customize its behavior and appearance through its properties. Each layout type offers a set of properties that control its spacing, margins, alignment, and stretching behavior. You can access and modify these properties in Qt Designer's Property Editor, allowing you to fine-tune the layout to achieve the desired visual effect.

Nesting Layouts for Complex UIs

For more complex user interfaces, you can nest layouts within each other, creating a hierarchical structure of containers and widgets. This enables you to organize your UI into logical sections and achieve intricate arrangements that adapt seamlessly to different window sizes and screen resolutions.

Layout Management Best Practices

To ensure optimal layout management and a responsive user interface, adhere to the following best practices:

- **Choose the right layout for the job:** Select the layout type that best suits the arrangement and behavior of your widgets.
- **Use layouts consistently:** Apply layouts to all widgets within a window or container to ensure a cohesive and predictable interface.
- **Set size policies appropriately:** Configure the size policies of your widgets to control their resizing behavior within layouts.
- **Leverage spacers and stretch factors:** Use spacers and stretch factors to distribute space within layouts and achieve the desired visual balance.
- **Test on different screen sizes and resolutions:** Ensure your layouts adapt gracefully to various display configurations.

Example

Let's illustrate the use of layouts with a simple example:

C++

```
QWidget* window = new QWidget;
QPushButton* button1 = new QPushButton("Button 1", window);
QPushButton* button2 = new QPushButton("Button 2", window);
```

```
QHBoxLayout* layout = new
QHBoxLayout(window);
layout->addWidget(button1);
layout->addWidget(button2);

window->show();
```

In this example, we create two push buttons and arrange them horizontally using a `QHBoxLayout`. The layout automatically distributes the available space between the buttons, ensuring a balanced and visually pleasing arrangement.

Qt's layout system is a powerful tool for creating responsive and adaptable user interfaces. By mastering the various layout types, properties, and best practices, you can craft GUIs that maintain their aesthetic appeal and usability across different platforms and devices.

Connecting Signals and Slots

At the heart of Qt's event-driven architecture lies the ingenious mechanism of signals and slots. This powerful paradigm enables seamless communication between objects within your application, facilitating dynamic and interactive user experiences. In this section, we'll delve into the intricacies of signals and slots, exploring their purpose, implementation, and pivotal role in orchestrating the behavior of your Qt GUI applications.

The Signal-Slot Symphony

Signals and slots form a harmonious duet, where signals act as messengers, broadcasting notifications of events or state changes, and slots act as attentive listeners, responding to these signals and executing corresponding actions. This decoupled communication model promotes loose coupling between objects, fostering modularity, flexibility, and maintainability in your code.

Signals: The Messengers

A signal is a special member function of a `QObject`-derived class that can be emitted to announce an event or state change. Signals carry no return values and can have any number of arguments, allowing them to convey rich information about the event that triggered them.

Qt provides a plethora of pre-defined signals for its built-in widgets and classes. For example, the `QPushButton` class emits a `clicked()` signal when the button is pressed, and the `QLineEdit` class emits a `textChanged()` signal whenever the text in the line edit is modified. You can also define custom signals in your own classes to communicate specific events relevant to your application's logic.

Slots: The Listeners

A slot is a regular member function of a `QObject`-derived class that can be connected to a signal. When a signal is emitted, any slots connected to it are automatically invoked, allowing them to respond to the event and execute appropriate actions.

Slots can have the same parameters as the signal they are connected to, enabling them to receive and process the information conveyed by the signal. You can connect multiple slots to a single signal, creating a chain of reactions that propagate throughout your application in response to a specific event.

The `connect()` Function: The Conductor

73

The `connect()` function acts as the conductor, orchestrating the connection between signals and slots. It establishes a link between a specific signal of an object and a corresponding slot of another object, ensuring that the slot is invoked whenever the signal is emitted.

The `connect()` function typically takes the following form:

C++

```
connect(sender, &SenderClass::signal, receiver, &ReceiverClass::slot);
```

Where:

- `sender`: The object emitting the signal.
- `&SenderClass::signal`: The signal to be connected.
- `receiver`: The object receiving the signal and executing the slot.
- `&ReceiverClass::slot`: The slot to be invoked when the signal is emitted.

Qt Designer Integration

Qt Designer streamlines the process of connecting signals and slots by providing a visual interface for establishing these connections. In the "Signal/Slot Editor," you can drag and drop connections between widgets, visually representing the flow of communication within your application.

Best Practices

To ensure effective and maintainable signal-slot connections, adhere to the following best practices:

- **Use descriptive signal and slot names:** Choose names that clearly convey the purpose and intent of the signal or slot.
- **Connect signals and slots in the constructor:** Establish connections early in the object's lifecycle to ensure they are active throughout its lifetime.
- **Disconnect signals and slots when no longer needed:** Prevent memory leaks and unintended behavior by disconnecting connections when they are no longer required.
- **Be mindful of signal-slot parameter compatibility:** Ensure that the parameters of the connected signal and slot match in type and order.

Signals and slots are the lifeblood of Qt's event-driven architecture, enabling seamless communication between objects and facilitating dynamic and interactive user experiences. By understanding the roles of signals, slots, and the `connect()` function, you can orchestrate the behavior of your Qt GUI applications with precision and elegance.

Compiling and Running Your Application

With your Qt project's user interface meticulously designed and the intricate web of signal-slot connections established, the moment of truth arrives: compiling and running your application. This pivotal step transforms your code and design into a tangible, interactive experience, allowing you to witness the fruits of your labor come to life. In this section, we'll guide you through the process of building and executing your Qt application, empowering you to share your creation with the world.

Building Your Project

Qt Creator streamlines the build process, automating the compilation and linking of your source code into an executable application. To initiate the build, simply click on the "Build" button in Qt Creator's toolbar or press `Ctrl+B`. Qt Creator will then invoke the selected build system (qmake or CMake) to transform your code into a binary executable.

During the build process, Qt Creator displays the build output in the "Compile Output" pane at the bottom of the window. This pane provides valuable information about the compilation progress, any encountered errors or warnings, and the overall build status.

Addressing Build Errors

If any errors occur during the build process, Qt Creator highlights them in the "Issues" pane, providing detailed descriptions and often suggesting potential solutions. Carefully review these errors, identify their root causes, and make the necessary corrections to your code. Once the errors are resolved, rebuild your project to ensure a successful compilation.

Running Your Application

With a successful build, your application is ready to be executed. Click on the green "Run" button in Qt Creator's toolbar or press `Ctrl+R`. Qt Creator will launch your application, presenting its main window and any associated widgets.

Interacting with Your GUI

Now comes the exciting part: interacting with your GUI! Click on buttons, enter text in input fields, navigate through menus, and explore the various elements you've meticulously designed. Observe how your application responds to user interactions, ensuring that the signal-slot connections trigger the expected actions and behaviors.

Debugging and Troubleshooting

If your application doesn't behave as expected or encounters unexpected errors during runtime, Qt Creator's debugging capabilities come to the rescue. Set breakpoints in your code, step through the execution line by line, inspect variable values, and identify the root causes of any issues. Qt Creator's debugger empowers you to diagnose and resolve problems efficiently, ensuring a smooth and polished user experience.

Deploying Your Application

Once you're satisfied with your application's functionality and stability, you can deploy it to other systems or share it with others. Qt Creator facilitates the deployment process by generating platform-specific executables and providing options to bundle necessary libraries and resources.

Compiling and running your Qt application is a gratifying milestone in the development process, marking the transition from code and design to a tangible and interactive experience. Qt Creator's build and run capabilities streamline this process, enabling you to iterate rapidly, identify and resolve issues, and ultimately deliver a polished and user-friendly application.

Part II: Mastering Qt Core Concepts

Chapter 4: Signals and Slots: The Heart of Qt Communication

Understanding the Signal-Slot Mechanism

At the core of Qt's elegant event-driven architecture lies the ingenious mechanism of signals and slots. This powerful paradigm revolutionizes the way objects communicate within your application, fostering loose coupling, modularity, and flexibility. In this section, we'll embark on a journey to unravel the inner workings of the signal-slot mechanism, shedding light on its conceptual foundation, practical implementation, and profound impact on Qt development.

The Essence of Signals and Slots

Signals and slots constitute a dynamic duo, where signals act as messengers, broadcasting notifications of events or state changes, and slots act as attentive listeners, responding to these signals and executing corresponding actions. This decoupled communication model liberates objects from direct dependencies, enabling them to interact indirectly through signals and slots, promoting a clean and maintainable code structure.

Signals: The Messengers

A signal is a special member function of a `QObject`-derived class that can be emitted to announce an event or state change. It acts as a beacon, radiating information about occurrences within an object to the wider application. Signals carry no return values, focusing solely on broadcasting notifications. However, they can have any number of arguments, allowing them to convey rich and detailed information about the event that triggered them.

Qt's extensive library of built-in classes comes equipped with a plethora of pre-defined signals, catering to a wide range of events and interactions. For instance, the `QPushButton` class emits a `clicked()` signal when the button is pressed, while the `QLineEdit` class emits a `textChanged()` signal whenever the text within the line edit is modified. These pre-defined signals provide a convenient way to respond to common user interactions and system events.

Moreover, Qt empowers you to define custom signals in your own classes, tailoring them to your application's specific needs. By emitting custom signals, you can communicate unique events or state changes that are relevant to your application's logic, fostering a highly modular and adaptable architecture.

Slots: The Listeners

On the receiving end of the signal-slot communication channel reside the slots. A slot is a regular member function of a `QObject`-derived class that can be connected to a signal. It acts as an attentive listener, poised to react and execute specific actions whenever a connected signal is emitted.

Slots can have the same parameters as the signal they are connected to, allowing them to seamlessly receive and process the information conveyed by the signal. This enables you to define precise and context-aware responses to events, tailoring your application's behavior to the specific circumstances.

Furthermore, you can connect multiple slots to a single signal, creating a chain reaction where each connected slot is invoked sequentially in response to the signal's emission. This cascading effect empowers you to orchestrate complex behaviors and interactions within your application, fostering a dynamic and responsive user experience.

The `connect()` Function: The Bridge

The `connect()` function serves as the bridge between signals and slots, establishing the vital link that enables communication. It acts as a conduit, channeling signals from emitting objects to their designated slot recipients.

The typical syntax of the `connect()` function is as follows:

C++

```
connect(sender, &SenderClass::signal, receiver, &ReceiverClass::slot);
```

In this concise yet powerful expression, we specify the `sender` object emitting the signal, the specific `signal` to be connected, the `receiver` object responsible for executing the slot, and the corresponding `slot` to be invoked. Once this connection is established, the `receiver`'s slot will be automatically called whenever the `sender` emits the specified signal.

The Magic Behind the Scenes

Under the hood, Qt's signal-slot mechanism leverages the Meta-Object Compiler (MOC), a preprocessor that generates additional code to facilitate the connections between signals and slots. The MOC scans your source code, identifies signals and slots, and creates the necessary infrastructure to enable their seamless interaction at runtime.

The signal-slot mechanism is the beating heart of Qt's event-driven architecture, infusing your applications with dynamism, interactivity, and responsiveness. By understanding the roles of signals, slots, and the `connect()` function, you gain the power to orchestrate complex communication patterns, respond to user interactions, and create GUI applications that feel alive and engaging.

Custom Signals and Slots

While Qt provides a rich collection of pre-defined signals and slots for its built-in widgets and classes, the true power of the signal-slot mechanism lies in its extensibility. Qt empowers you to define custom signals and slots in your own classes, tailoring them to your application's unique communication needs. In this section, we'll explore the art of crafting custom signals and slots, unlocking a new dimension of flexibility and expressiveness in your Qt projects.

Declaring Custom Signals

To declare a custom signal in your class, you utilize the `signals` keyword within the class definition. The syntax is straightforward:

C++

```
class MyClass : public QObject {
    Q_OBJECT // Necessary for signals and slots

public:
    // ... other class members ...

signals:
    void myCustomSignal(int value);
};
```

In this example, we declare a custom signal named `myCustomSignal` that carries an integer value. The `signals` keyword designates this function as a signal, and the `Q_OBJECT` macro is essential for enabling the Meta-Object Compiler (MOC) to process signals and slots in your class.

Emitting Custom Signals

Once a custom signal is declared, you can emit it from within your class's member functions using the `emit` keyword. This triggers the signal-slot mechanism, notifying any connected slots and passing the specified arguments.

C++

```
void MyClass::someFunction() {
        int calculatedValue = 42; // Perform some calculations

        emit myCustomSignal(calculatedValue);
}
```

In this snippet, we emit the `myCustomSignal` with the calculated value, broadcasting this information to any connected slots.

Defining Custom Slots

Custom slots are defined using the `slots` keyword within your class definition. They are regular member functions that can be connected to signals, both pre-defined and custom.

C++

```
class MyOtherClass : public QObject {
    Q_OBJECT

public:
    // ... other class members ...

public slots:
    void handleCustomSignal(int value)
{
        qDebug() << "Received custom signal with value:" << value;
        // Perform actions based on the received value
    }
};
```

In this example, we define a custom slot named `handleCustomSignal` that accepts an integer value. This slot can be connected to the `myCustomSignal` emitted by `MyClass`, allowing `MyOtherClass` to respond to the signal and process the received value.

Connecting Custom Signals and Slots

Connecting custom signals and slots follows the same pattern as connecting pre-defined signals and slots. You utilize the `connect()` function, specifying the sender object, the custom signal, the receiver object, and the custom slot.

C++

```
MyClass* myObject = new MyClass;
MyOtherClass* otherObject = new MyOtherClass;

connect(myObject,
&MyClass::myCustomSignal, otherObject,
&MyOtherClass::handleCustomSignal);
```

With this connection established, whenever `myObject` emits the `myCustomSignal`, `otherObject`'s `handleCustomSignal` slot will be invoked, receiving the emitted value and performing the corresponding actions.

The Power of Custom Signals and Slots

Custom signals and slots unlock a world of possibilities in Qt development. They empower you to:

- **Create modular and decoupled components:** Objects can communicate indirectly through signals and slots, reducing dependencies and promoting code reusability.
- **Implement custom event handling:** Define and emit signals to represent specific events within your application, triggering custom actions in response.
- **Build flexible and adaptable architectures:** Objects can dynamically connect and disconnect signals and slots at runtime, enabling adaptable and responsive behaviors.
- **Enhance code readability and maintainability:** Signals and slots provide a clear and intuitive way to express

communication patterns within your application.

Custom signals and slots are a testament to the flexibility and extensibility of Qt's signal-slot mechanism. By defining your own signals and slots, you gain fine-grained control over communication within your application, fostering modularity, adaptability, and maintainability. As you progress through this book, you'll witness the power of custom signals and slots in action, enabling you to create sophisticated and interactive GUI applications that cater to your unique requirements. Embrace this powerful tool, and let it elevate your Qt development to new heights.

Connecting Signals and Slots Programmatically

While Qt Designer offers a visual and intuitive way to connect signals and slots, there are scenarios where programmatic connections become necessary or even advantageous. This approach provides greater flexibility, enabling dynamic connections at runtime, conditional connections based on application logic, and seamless integration with code-driven UI construction. In this section, we'll explore the art of connecting signals and slots programmatically, empowering you to wield this technique with finesse and precision in your Qt projects.

The `connect()` Function: Your Trusty Companion

At the heart of programmatic signal-slot connections lies the `connect()` function, a versatile tool that establishes the link between a signal and a slot. Its signature, while seemingly simple, encapsulates the essence of Qt's communication paradigm:

C++

```
bool QObject::connect(const QObject *sender, const char *signal, const QObject *receiver, const char *method, Qt::ConnectionType type = Qt::AutoConnection);
```

Let's dissect its components:

- `sender`: The object emitting the signal.
- `signal`: The name of the signal to be connected, specified as a string.

- `receiver`: The object receiving the signal and executing the slot.
- `method`: The name of the slot to be invoked when the signal is emitted, also specified as a string.
- `type`: (Optional) The connection type, governing the timing and threading behavior of the signal-slot invocation.

Establishing the Connection

To connect a signal and a slot programmatically, you invoke the `connect()` function, providing the necessary arguments. Qt's Meta-Object Compiler (MOC) works its magic behind the scenes, ensuring that the connection is established correctly and the slot is invoked whenever the signal is emitted.

C++

```
QPushButton* button = new QPushButton("Click me!");
QObject::connect(button, "clicked()", this, "onButtonClicked()");
```

In this example, we connect the `clicked()` signal of a `QPushButton` to the `onButtonClicked()` slot of the current object (`this`). When the button is clicked, the `onButtonClicked()` slot will be executed.

Advanced Connection Types

Qt offers several connection types that influence the timing and threading behavior of signal-slot invocations:

- `Qt::AutoConnection` (default): Qt determines the connection type automatically based on the thread affinity of the sender and receiver objects.
- `Qt::DirectConnection`: The slot is invoked immediately when the signal is emitted, even if the sender and receiver are in different threads.
- `Qt::QueuedConnection`: The slot is invoked asynchronously in the receiver's thread when control returns to the event loop.
- `Qt::BlockingQueuedConnection`: Similar to `Qt::QueuedConnection`, but the emitting thread blocks until the slot is executed.

Choose the appropriate connection type based on your application's requirements and the desired behavior of the signal-slot communication.

Dynamic Connections

One of the strengths of programmatic connections is the ability to establish and disconnect connections dynamically at runtime. This empowers you to create flexible and adaptable applications that respond to changing conditions and user interactions.

C++

```
if (someCondition) {
          QObject::connect(object1,
"signal1()", object2, "slot1()");
} else {
          QObject::disconnect(object1,
"signal1()", object2, "slot1()");
}
```

In this example, we conditionally connect or disconnect a signal and a slot based on the value of `someCondition`. This dynamic behavior allows your application to adapt its communication patterns based on its internal state or external events.

Connecting signals and slots programmatically provides a powerful and flexible approach to managing communication within your Qt applications. By leveraging the `connect()` function and understanding the various connection types, you can establish dynamic connections, respond to events in a precise and context-aware manner, and build adaptable architectures that cater to your application's unique requirements.

Advanced Signal-Slot Techniques

While the fundamental concepts of signals and slots provide a solid foundation for communication in Qt applications, mastering advanced techniques can unlock new levels of flexibility, efficiency, and expressiveness in your code. In this section, we'll explore some of these techniques, empowering you to wield the full power of the signal-slot mechanism and craft sophisticated GUI applications that respond dynamically to user interactions and system events.

Lambda Expressions: Concise and Expressive Connections

Lambda expressions, introduced in C++11, offer a concise and elegant way to connect signals and slots, especially for simple or one-off connections. They allow you to define anonymous functions directly within the `connect()` call, eliminating the need for separate named slot functions and promoting code clarity.

C++

```
QPushButton* button = new QPushButton("Click me!");
connect(button, &QPushButton::clicked, [this]() {
    QMessageBox::information(this, "Button Clicked", "You clicked the button!");
});
```

In this example, we connect the `clicked()` signal of a `QPushButton` to a lambda expression that displays a message box when the button is clicked.

The lambda expression captures the `this` pointer, allowing it to access the parent widget and display the message box correctly.

Overloaded Signals and Slots

Qt allows you to define multiple signals or slots with the same name but different parameter lists within a class. This technique, known as overloading, enables you to handle different variations of an event or action based on the specific arguments passed.

C++

```
class MyClass : public QObject {
    Q_OBJECT

public:
    // ... other class members ...

signals:
    void valueChanged(int newValue);
            void    valueChanged(double newValue);

public slots:
        void   handleIntValueChanged(int newValue);
```

```
                                              void
handleDoubleValueChanged(double
newValue);
};
```

In this example, we define two overloaded signals named `valueChanged`, one accepting an integer and the other accepting a double. We also define corresponding overloaded slots to handle each signal variation. This allows us to respond differently based on the type of value that has changed.

Custom Signal-Slot Argument Types

While Qt's built-in signals and slots typically use basic data types or Qt-specific classes as arguments, you can also define custom types for your signals and slots. This enables you to pass complex data structures or custom objects between objects, facilitating more sophisticated communication patterns.

To use custom types in signals and slots, you need to register them with Qt's Meta-Object System using the `qRegisterMetaType()` function.

C++

```
struct MyCustomData {
    // ... data members ...
};

qRegisterMetaType<MyCustomData>("MyCustomData");

class MyClass : public QObject {
    Q_OBJECT

public:
    // ... other class members ...

signals:
        void  customDataChanged(const MyCustomData& newData);

public slots:
    void handleCustomDataChanged(const MyCustomData& newData);
};
```

In this example, we define a custom struct `MyCustomData` and register it as a meta-type. We then declare a signal `customDataChanged` that carries a `MyCustomData` object and a corresponding slot to handle it.

Mastering advanced signal-slot techniques empowers you to harness the full potential of Qt's communication paradigm. By leveraging lambda expressions, overloaded signals and slots, and custom argument types, you can create flexible, adaptable, and expressive connections that facilitate complex interactions and dynamic behaviors within your GUI applications. As you continue your Qt journey, explore these techniques and experiment with their applications to elevate your development skills and craft user interfaces that are both powerful and intuitive.

Chapter 5: Layouts: Organizing Your GUI

Built-in Layout Managers

In the realm of Qt GUI development, achieving a visually harmonious and adaptable interface demands more than just scattering widgets across the canvas. It necessitates a structured and organized approach to arranging these widgets, ensuring they seamlessly adjust to various window sizes and screen resolutions. Qt's arsenal of built-in layout managers emerges as the solution, providing an elegant and efficient means to orchestrate the placement and resizing of widgets within your user interfaces. In this section, we'll delve into the intricacies of these layout managers, exploring their unique characteristics, properties, and applications in crafting visually pleasing and responsive GUIs.

QHBoxLayout: Horizontal Harmony

The `QHBoxLayout` class arranges its child widgets horizontally in a single row, flowing from left to right. It excels in scenarios where you need to present elements sequentially, such as a toolbar with buttons or a form with labels and input fields aligned horizontally. The layout automatically distributes the available horizontal space among its widgets, ensuring a balanced and aesthetically pleasing arrangement.

You can customize the spacing between widgets, set margins around the layout, and control the alignment of widgets within the layout using its properties. Furthermore, you can assign stretch factors to individual widgets, influencing their relative sizes when the layout is resized.

QVBoxLayout: Vertical Virtuosity

The `QVBoxLayout` class, the vertical counterpart to `QHBoxLayout`, arranges its child widgets vertically in a single column, flowing from top to bottom. It's ideal for scenarios where you need to present elements in a stacked fashion, such as a list of items or a series of stacked panels. Like `QHBoxLayout`, `QVBoxLayout` automatically manages the vertical space distribution and offers properties for customization and fine-tuning.

QGridLayout: Grid-like Precision

The `QGridLayout` class introduces a grid-like structure for arranging widgets, dividing the available space into rows and columns. Each widget can occupy one or more cells within the grid, providing greater flexibility and control over widget placement. `QGridLayout` is particularly useful for complex layouts with multiple elements that need to be aligned both horizontally and vertically.

You can specify the row and column span for each widget, control the spacing and margins between cells, and align widgets within their respective cells. `QGridLayout`'s adaptability makes it suitable for a wide range of UI designs, from calculators and calendars to image galleries and data grids.

QFormLayout: Formidable Organization

The `QFormLayout` class specializes in creating two-column layouts, typically used for forms or data entry interfaces. It automatically pairs labels with their corresponding input widgets, ensuring a clear and organized presentation of information. `QFormLayout` simplifies the creation of forms, handling label alignment, widget spacing, and overall layout structure.

You can customize the appearance of labels, adjust the spacing between rows, and control the stretching behavior of widgets within the layout. `QFormLayout`'s focus on form-like structures makes it an invaluable tool for building user-friendly and efficient data input interfaces.

Choosing the Right Layout

Selecting the appropriate layout manager depends on the specific requirements of your user interface. Consider the following factors:

- **Widget arrangement:** Do you need to arrange widgets horizontally, vertically, in a grid, or in a form-like structure?
- **Space distribution:** How should the available space be distributed among the widgets?
- **Resizing behavior:** How should the widgets resize when the window or container is resized?
- **Visual aesthetics:** What visual style and layout are you aiming to achieve?

By carefully evaluating these factors and experimenting with different layout combinations, you can create interfaces that are both visually appealing and functionally effective.

Qt's built-in layout managers provide a powerful and flexible framework for organizing your GUI widgets. By harnessing the capabilities of `QHBoxLayout`, `QVBoxLayout`, `QGridLayout`, and `QFormLayout`, you can craft user interfaces that are not only visually pleasing but also adaptable and responsive to different screen sizes and resolutions.

Custom Layouts

While Qt's built-in layout managers provide a solid foundation for organizing widgets, there are scenarios where their capabilities might fall short of your specific design requirements. In such cases, Qt empowers you to create custom layouts, tailored precisely to your needs. This advanced technique grants you unparalleled control over widget placement, resizing behavior, and overall layout structure, enabling you to craft unique and visually captivating user interfaces. In this section, we'll embark on a journey into the realm of custom layouts, exploring their creation, implementation, and application in pushing the boundaries of Qt GUI design.

The Essence of Custom Layouts

At its core, a custom layout in Qt is a subclass of the `QLayout` class, inheriting its core functionalities and extending them with your own specialized logic. By overriding key virtual functions, you gain the ability to dictate how child widgets are sized, positioned, and arranged within the layout.

Creating a Custom Layout

To create a custom layout, follow these steps:

1. **Subclass** `QLayout`: Create a new class that inherits from `QLayout`.
2. **Implement Virtual Functions:** Override the following key virtual functions:
    - `sizeHint()`: Returns the preferred size of the layout.
    - `minimumSize()`: Returns the minimum size the layout can be shrunk to.
    - `setGeometry()`: Sets the geometry of the layout and its child widgets.
3. **Add Widgets:** Provide a mechanism for adding child widgets to the layout.
4. **Handle Events:** Implement event handlers to respond to resize events and other relevant events.

Example: A Simple Custom Layout

Let's illustrate the creation of a custom layout with a simplified example:

C++

```
class MyCustomLayout : public QLayout
```

```cpp
{
    Q_OBJECT

public:
    MyCustomLayout(QWidget *parent = nullptr);
    ~MyCustomLayout();

    void addItem(QLayoutItem *item) override;
    QSize sizeHint() const override;
    QSize minimumSize() const override;
    void setGeometry(const QRect &rect) override;

private:
    QList<QLayoutItem *> itemList;
};
```

In this example, we define a custom layout class `MyCustomLayout` that inherits from `QLayout`. We override the necessary virtual functions and provide a simple mechanism for adding child widgets using the `addItem()` function.

Implementing Layout Logic

The heart of a custom layout lies in the implementation of its virtual functions. The `sizeHint()` function calculates the preferred size of the layout based on the size hints of its child widgets. The `minimumSize()` function determines the minimum size the layout can be shrunk to while still accommodating its child widgets. The `setGeometry()` function is responsible for setting the geometry of the layout and its child widgets, ensuring they are positioned and sized correctly within the available space.

The implementation of these functions will vary depending on the specific layout logic you want to achieve. You have complete freedom to define how child widgets are arranged, resized, and positioned within your custom layout.

Applying Custom Layouts

Once you've created a custom layout, you can apply it to widgets in your Qt application, just like you would with built-in layouts. You can use it programmatically or visually within Qt Designer, providing a seamless integration into your development workflow.

Custom layouts empower you to transcend the limitations of built-in layout managers, enabling you to craft unique and visually captivating user interfaces. By subclassing `QLayout` and implementing your own layout logic, you gain unparalleled control over widget arrangement, resizing behavior, and overall layout structure.

Responsive Design with Layouts

In today's multi-device world, where users interact with applications on a diverse range of screens, from expansive desktops to compact smartphones, crafting responsive user interfaces is paramount. A responsive design ensures that your GUI adapts gracefully to different screen sizes and resolutions, providing an optimal user experience regardless of the device being used. Qt's layout system, with its built-in and custom layout managers, empowers you to achieve responsive design with elegance and efficiency. In this section, we'll explore the strategies and techniques for creating layouts that seamlessly adapt to various screen configurations, ensuring your Qt applications shine on any device.

Embrace the Power of Layouts

Qt's layout system forms the cornerstone of responsive design. By utilizing layouts effectively, you can create interfaces that dynamically adjust their widget arrangements, sizes, and positions in response to changes in the available space. This adaptability ensures that your GUI remains visually appealing and functional, regardless of the screen dimensions or orientation.

Leverage Layout Properties

Qt layouts offer a wealth of properties that enable you to fine-tune their behavior and achieve responsive design. Let's explore some key properties:

- **Size Constraints:** Each widget within a layout can have minimum, maximum, and preferred size constraints. By setting these constraints appropriately, you can control how widgets resize and ensure they maintain their usability even in confined spaces.
- **Size Policies:** Size policies dictate how widgets expand or shrink within a layout. You can set horizontal and vertical size policies for each widget, influencing their resizing behavior in response to changes in the layout's dimensions.

- **Stretch Factors:** Stretch factors determine the relative distribution of space among widgets within a layout. By assigning different stretch factors to widgets, you can control their proportional resizing and ensure a balanced visual composition.
- **Spacing and Margins:** Layouts allow you to customize the spacing between widgets and the margins around the layout itself. These properties contribute to the visual aesthetics and readability of your interface.

Nesting Layouts for Adaptability

For complex user interfaces, nesting layouts within each other can be a powerful strategy for achieving responsive design. By creating a hierarchy of layouts, you can divide your UI into logical sections that can be rearranged, resized, or even hidden based on the available screen space.

For example, you might use a `QVBoxLayout` to arrange a header, a content area, and a footer vertically. Within the content area, you might employ a `QHBoxLayout` to arrange elements horizontally on larger screens, but switch to a `QVBoxLayout` on smaller screens to stack the elements vertically. This nesting of layouts allows your UI to adapt seamlessly to different screen sizes, providing an optimal user experience on any device.

Media Queries: Conditional Styling

Qt's style sheet system supports media queries, enabling you to apply different styles to your widgets based on specific conditions, such as screen width, height, or orientation. This empowers you to tailor the appearance of your UI to different screen configurations, further enhancing its responsiveness.

For instance, you might use a media query to apply a larger font size to labels on larger screens, ensuring readability even from a distance. Or you might use a media query to hide certain widgets or rearrange layouts on smaller screens, optimizing the interface for limited space.

Testing and Iteration

Thorough testing across a variety of devices and screen sizes is crucial for ensuring a truly responsive design. Use Qt Creator's device emulator or test your application on physical devices to identify any layout issues or usability concerns. Iterate on your design based on your findings, refining the layout properties, widget arrangements, and media queries until your GUI delivers an exceptional experience on any screen.

Responsive design is an essential aspect of modern GUI development, ensuring that your applications adapt gracefully to the diverse landscape of devices and screen sizes. Qt's layout system, with its built-in and custom layout managers, empowers you to achieve responsive design with elegance and efficiency. By leveraging layout properties, nesting layouts strategically, and utilizing media queries, you can craft user interfaces that shine on any screen, providing an optimal user experience regardless of the device being used.

Best Practices for Layout Management

Effectively managing layouts is crucial for creating user interfaces that are both visually appealing and functionally robust. Qt's layout system offers a powerful framework for organizing widgets, but mastering its nuances requires adherence to best practices. In this section, we'll distill the wisdom accumulated from countless Qt projects, presenting you with a set of guidelines that will elevate your layout management skills and empower you to craft exceptional GUI applications.

1. **Choose the Right Layout for the Job**

Qt provides a diverse array of layout managers, each with its own strengths and ideal use cases. Selecting the appropriate layout is paramount for achieving the desired arrangement and behavior of your widgets. Consider the following:

- `QHBoxLayout` **and** `QVBoxLayout`: Ideal for simple horizontal or vertical arrangements of widgets.
- `QGridLayout`: Perfect for complex layouts with multiple elements that need to be aligned both horizontally and vertically.
- `QFormLayout`: Tailored for forms or data entry interfaces, automatically pairing labels with input widgets.
- **Custom Layouts**: When built-in layouts fall short, create custom layouts to achieve precise control over widget placement and resizing.

2. **Use Layouts Consistently**

Apply layouts to all widgets within a window or container to ensure a cohesive and predictable interface. Avoid mixing layouts within the same container, as this can lead to unexpected behavior and visual inconsistencies. By adhering to a consistent layout strategy, you create a sense of order and harmony in your UI.

3. **Set Size Policies Appropriately**

Size policies govern how widgets resize within a layout. Each widget has both a horizontal and a vertical size policy, which can be set to one of the following values:

- `QSizePolicy::Fixed`: The widget's size remains fixed and does not change when the layout is resized.
- `QSizePolicy::Minimum`: The widget's size is at least its minimum size hint but can grow to accommodate its contents or the available space.
- `QSizePolicy::Maximum`: The widget's size is at most its maximum size hint but can shrink to accommodate its contents or the available space.
- `QSizePolicy::Preferred`: The widget's size is ideally its preferred size hint but can grow or shrink to accommodate its contents or the available space.

- `QSizePolicy::Expanding`: The widget expands to fill all available space within the layout.

Choose size policies carefully to control how widgets resize and ensure they maintain their usability and visual appeal across different screen configurations.

4. **Leverage Spacers and Stretch Factors**

Spacers and stretch factors provide additional control over space distribution within layouts. Spacers are invisible widgets that occupy space within a layout, allowing you to create gaps between other widgets. Stretch factors, assigned to individual widgets, influence their relative sizes when the layout is resized.

By strategically using spacers and stretch factors, you can achieve balanced and visually pleasing layouts, even when the available space changes.

5. **Nest Layouts Strategically**

For complex UIs, nesting layouts within each other can enhance organization and adaptability. By creating a hierarchy of layouts, you can group related widgets together and control their collective behavior within the overall interface.

When nesting layouts, be mindful of the interplay between parent and child layouts. Ensure that size policies and stretch factors are set appropriately to avoid conflicts and achieve the desired resizing behavior.

6. **Test on Different Screen Sizes and Resolutions**

Thorough testing across a variety of devices and screen configurations is crucial for ensuring a truly responsive design. Use Qt Creator's device emulator or test your application on physical devices to identify any layout issues or usability concerns. Iterate on your design based on your findings, refining layout properties, widget arrangements, and nesting strategies until your GUI delivers an optimal experience on any screen.

7. **Embrace the Power of Qt Designer**

Qt Designer provides a visual and intuitive interface for working with layouts. Leverage its drag-and-drop functionality, property editor, and real-time preview to experiment with different layout configurations and fine-tune your UI design.

8. Stay Informed about Qt's Layout Evolution

Qt's layout system continues to evolve, with new features and enhancements introduced in each release. Stay abreast of the latest developments by consulting the Qt documentation and exploring online resources. By staying informed, you can leverage the full power of Qt's layout capabilities and create cutting-edge user interfaces.

Mastering layout management is essential for building responsive and visually appealing Qt GUI applications. By adhering to best practices, leveraging layout properties, nesting layouts strategically, and testing thoroughly, you can create interfaces that adapt gracefully to different screen configurations and deliver an exceptional user experience on any device.

Chapter 6: Widgets: The Building Blocks of Your GUI

Essential Qt Widgets

In the realm of Qt GUI development, widgets reign supreme as the fundamental visual elements that breathe life into your user interfaces. These versatile components encapsulate a wide range of functionalities, from simple buttons and labels to complex tables and tree views. Qt's extensive library of pre-built widgets empowers you to construct intuitive and engaging interfaces that seamlessly connect with your users. In this section, we'll embark on a journey to explore the essential Qt widgets, unraveling their capabilities, properties, and applications in crafting captivating GUI experiences.

Buttons: Triggering Actions

Buttons are the quintessential interactive elements in any GUI, enabling users to initiate actions and commands within your application. Qt offers a variety of button widgets, each catering to specific use cases:

- `QPushButton`: The most common button type, `QPushButton` displays clickable text or icons. It supports various styles and customization options, allowing you to create visually appealing and informative buttons.
- `QToolButton`: Designed for toolbars and menus, `QToolButton` typically displays icons and can be configured to trigger actions or display popup menus.
- `QRadioButton`: Presents a group of mutually exclusive options, allowing users to select only one choice at a time.
- `QCheckBox`: Enables users to toggle options on or off, ideal for settings or preferences where multiple selections are possible.

Labels: Displaying Information

Labels serve as informative elements within your GUI, displaying text or images to convey messages, instructions, or status updates. Qt's `QLabel` widget offers a straightforward way to incorporate labels into your interfaces.

You can customize a label's text, font, color, alignment, and word wrap behavior to achieve the desired visual presentation. `QLabel` also supports rich text formatting, enabling you to display styled text with different fonts, colors, and hyperlinks.

Text Edits: Input and Output

Text edits facilitate user input and display textual information within your GUI. Qt provides several text edit widgets, catering to different input scenarios:

- `QLineEdit`: A single-line text edit, ideal for capturing short inputs like names, email addresses, or search queries. It supports features like password masking, input validation, and auto-completion.
- `QTextEdit`: A multi-line text edit, suitable for capturing longer text inputs like descriptions, comments, or code snippets. It supports rich text formatting and basic editing capabilities.
- `QPlainTextEdit`: A specialized text edit optimized for handling plain text, offering improved performance for large documents or code editing.

Combo Boxes: Efficient Selection

Combo boxes present a dropdown list of options for users to select from. They offer a space-efficient alternative to radio buttons or checkboxes when you have multiple choices. Qt's `QComboBox` widget provides a user-friendly way to incorporate combo boxes into your interfaces.

You can populate a combo box with items programmatically or through Qt Designer. `QComboBox` supports features like editable text input, custom item delegates for visual customization, and signal-slot connections to handle item selection events.

Sliders and Progress Bars: Visual Feedback

Sliders and progress bars offer visual representations of continuous values or the progress of ongoing tasks, providing valuable feedback to users.

- `QSlider`: Enables users to select a value within a specified range by moving a handle along a track. It's commonly used for adjusting volume, brightness, or other continuous settings.
- `QProgressBar`: Displays the progress of a task or operation, typically represented by a filled bar or a percentage value. It's ideal for keeping users informed during lengthy processes.

Tables and Tree Views: Structured Data

Tables and tree views present structured data in an organized and navigable manner, facilitating efficient data exploration and manipulation.

- QTableWidget: Displays data in a tabular format with rows and columns. It supports sorting, filtering, and editing, making it suitable for presenting and managing large datasets.
- QTreeWidget: Presents hierarchical data in a tree-like structure with expandable and collapsible branches. It allows users to navigate through the data hierarchy and interact with individual items.

Qt's essential widgets provide the building blocks for crafting intuitive and engaging user interfaces. From buttons and labels to text edits, combo boxes, sliders, progress bars, tables, and tree views, these widgets empower you to create GUIs that are both visually appealing and functionally rich.

Custom Widgets

While Qt's extensive library of pre-built widgets caters to a wide range of GUI elements, there are scenarios where you need to create unique and specialized components that go beyond the capabilities of the standard offerings. Qt empowers you to craft custom widgets, tailored precisely to your application's specific requirements. In this section, we'll embark on a journey to explore the art of custom widget creation, unraveling the techniques, considerations, and best practices involved in building these bespoke components.

The Essence of Custom Widgets

At its core, a custom widget in Qt is a subclass of an existing Qt widget or, in some cases, a direct subclass of `QWidget`. By inheriting from a base widget, you gain access to its existing properties, methods, and signals, while also having the freedom to extend its functionality, modify its appearance, and tailor its behavior to your precise needs.

Creating a Custom Widget

The process of creating a custom widget typically involves the following steps:

1. **Choose a Base Class:** Select an appropriate base class for your custom widget. If you're building a widget with a

visual representation, consider inheriting from `QWidget` or one of its subclasses, such as `QLabel`, `QPushButton`, or `QFrame`. If your widget focuses on non-visual functionality, you might inherit from `QObject` or another suitable base class.
2. **Subclass the Base Class:** Create a new class that inherits from the chosen base class. This new class will represent your custom widget.
3. **Implement Constructor and Destructor:** Define the constructor and destructor for your custom widget. The constructor is responsible for initializing the widget's properties and setting up its initial state. The destructor handles any necessary cleanup when the widget is destroyed.
4. **Override Paint Event:** If your custom widget has a visual representation, override the `paintEvent()` function to draw its contents on the screen. This function is called whenever the widget needs to be repainted, allowing you to customize its appearance dynamically.
5. **Add Properties and Methods:** Define additional properties and methods specific to your custom widget's functionality. These might include functions to manipulate the

widget's data, handle user interactions, or emit custom signals.
6. **Implement Event Handlers:** If your custom widget needs to respond to specific events, such as mouse clicks or keyboard presses, implement the corresponding event handler functions. These functions allow you to capture and process events, triggering appropriate actions within your widget.

Example: A Custom Progress Bar

Let's illustrate the creation of a custom widget with a simplified example:

C++

```
class MyProgressBar : public QWidget
{
    Q_OBJECT

public:
    explicit MyProgressBar(QWidget *parent = nullptr);
    ~MyProgressBar();

    void setValue(int value);

protected:
```

```
    void paintEvent(QPaintEvent *event) override;

private:
    int m_value;
};
```

In this example, we define a custom progress bar widget `MyProgressBar` that inherits from `QWidget`. We provide a `setValue()` function to update the progress bar's value and override the `paintEvent()` function to draw the progress bar's visual representation.

Considerations for Custom Widgets

When designing and implementing custom widgets, keep the following considerations in mind:

- **Modularity and Reusability:** Strive to create widgets that are self-contained and reusable across different projects. Encapsulate functionality within the widget itself, minimizing dependencies on external code.

- **Clarity and Maintainability:** Write clean and well-documented code, adhering to Qt's coding conventions and best practices. This ensures that your custom widgets are easy to understand, modify, and maintain.
- **Performance and Efficiency:** Optimize your custom widget's implementation to ensure it performs well, especially when handling large datasets or complex interactions.
- **Accessibility:** Design your custom widgets with accessibility in mind, ensuring they can be used by individuals with disabilities.

Custom widgets empower you to transcend the limitations of Qt's pre-built components, enabling you to create unique and specialized GUI elements that perfectly match your application's requirements. By subclassing existing widgets or inheriting directly from `QWidget`, you gain the flexibility to extend functionality, modify appearance, and tailor behavior to your precise needs.

Styling Widgets with Stylesheets

While Qt's built-in widgets offer a solid foundation for GUI development, their default appearance might not always align perfectly with your application's aesthetic vision. Qt's stylesheet system emerges as a powerful tool for customizing the look and feel of your widgets, enabling you to create visually stunning and cohesive interfaces that reflect your brand or design preferences. In this section, we'll delve into the art of styling widgets with stylesheets, exploring their syntax, capabilities, and application in transforming the visual landscape of your Qt applications.

The Language of Stylesheets

Qt stylesheets employ a syntax reminiscent of CSS (Cascading Style Sheets), a language widely used for styling web pages. This familiarity makes it relatively easy for developers with web development experience to grasp the concepts and apply them to Qt widgets.

A stylesheet consists of a series of rules, each targeting specific widget types or individual widgets. Each rule comprises a selector and a declaration block. The selector identifies the target widget(s), while the declaration block specifies the styles to be applied.

Selectors: Targeting Widgets

Qt stylesheets offer a variety of selectors to precisely target the widgets you want to style. Some common selectors include:

- **Type Selector:** Targets all widgets of a specific type. For example, `QPushButton` targets all push button widgets.
- **Class Selector:** Targets widgets that have a specific class name assigned to them. For example, `.myButtonClass` targets all widgets with the class name "myButtonClass."
- **ID Selector:** Targets a specific widget with a unique ID. For example, `#myButton` targets the widget with the ID "myButton."
- **Descendant Selector:** Targets widgets that are descendants of another widget. For example, `QWidget QPushButton` targets all push button widgets that are descendants of a `QWidget`.

Declaration Blocks: Defining Styles

The declaration block within a stylesheet rule specifies the styles to be applied to the targeted widgets. It consists of one or more property-value pairs, enclosed in curly braces.

CSS

```
QPushButton {
    background-color: blue;
    color: white;
    border-radius: 5px;
}
```

In this example, we target all `QPushButton` widgets and apply a blue background color, white text color, and rounded corners with a 5-pixel radius.

Properties: A Wealth of Customization

Qt stylesheets offer a vast array of properties that you can manipulate to customize the appearance of your widgets. These properties encompass:

- **Colors:** Control the background color, text color, border color, and other color attributes of widgets.
- **Fonts:** Specify the font family, size, weight, and style for text elements within widgets.
- **Borders:** Define the style, width, and color of borders around widgets.
- **Margins and Padding:** Control the spacing around and within widgets.

- **Images:** Set background images or icons for widgets.
- **Positioning:** Influence the positioning and alignment of widgets within layouts.
- **Animations and Transitions:** Create dynamic and visually engaging effects.

Applying Stylesheets

You can apply stylesheets to your Qt application in two primary ways:

1. **Programmatically:** Use the `setStyleSheet()` function to set a stylesheet for a specific widget or the entire application.

C++

```
QPushButton* button = new QPushButton("Styled Button");
button->setStyleSheet("background-color: green; color: yellow;");
```

2. **Qt Designer Integration:** Within Qt Designer, you can access the "Stylesheet" property in the Property Editor for each widget or the main window. This allows you

to apply styles directly within the design environment.

Best Practices

To ensure effective and maintainable stylesheet usage, adhere to the following best practices:

- **Use external stylesheet files:** Store your stylesheets in separate `.qss` files for better organization and reusability across multiple projects.
- **Organize your stylesheets:** Group related styles together and use comments to enhance readability and maintainability.
- **Leverage inheritance and cascading:** Utilize stylesheet inheritance and cascading to apply styles efficiently and avoid repetition.
- **Test on different platforms and styles:** Ensure your stylesheets render correctly across different operating systems and Qt styles.
- **Strive for consistency:** Maintain a consistent visual language throughout your application to create a cohesive and professional user experience.

Qt's stylesheet system empowers you to transcend the limitations of default widget appearances, enabling you to craft visually stunning and personalized interfaces that reflect your unique design vision. By mastering the language of stylesheets, exploring its vast array of properties, and adhering to best practices, you can transform the visual landscape of your Qt applications and create GUI experiences that captivate and engage your users.

Accessibility and Widgets

In the realm of GUI development, accessibility is not merely a buzzword; it's a fundamental principle that ensures your applications are inclusive and usable by individuals with disabilities. Qt embraces accessibility, providing a robust framework for creating interfaces that cater to a diverse range of users, including those with visual, auditory, motor, or cognitive impairments. In this section, we'll explore the importance of accessibility in Qt development, delve into Qt's accessibility features, and equip you with the knowledge and tools to build widgets that are both functional and inclusive.

The Imperative of Accessibility

Accessibility is not just a moral obligation; it's also a legal requirement in many countries. By designing accessible interfaces, you not only expand your application's reach and potential user base but also contribute to a more inclusive and equitable digital landscape.

Qt's commitment to accessibility manifests in its comprehensive support for assistive technologies, such as screen readers, magnifiers, and alternative input devices. By adhering to accessibility guidelines and leveraging Qt's built-in features, you can ensure that your widgets are perceivable, operable, understandable, and robust, catering to the diverse needs of your users.

Qt's Accessibility Framework

Qt's accessibility framework provides a bridge between your application and assistive technologies, enabling seamless communication and interaction. It encompasses several key components:

1. **Accessibility Objects:** Each widget in your Qt application is represented by an accessibility object, an instance of the `QAccessibleInterface` class. This object encapsulates information about the widget's

role, state, properties, and actions, making it accessible to assistive technologies.
2. **Accessibility Events:** Qt widgets emit accessibility events whenever their state or properties change. These events, such as focus changes, value changes, or text updates, notify assistive technologies about the dynamic nature of your interface, enabling them to provide real-time feedback to users.
3. **Keyboard Navigation:** Qt supports keyboard navigation, allowing users to interact with your widgets using only the keyboard. This is crucial for individuals with motor impairments who might have difficulty using a mouse or other pointing devices.
4. **Screen Reader Support:** Qt provides comprehensive support for screen readers, software applications that convert on-screen content into synthesized speech or braille output. By providing descriptive text alternatives for visual elements and ensuring proper focus management, you can make your widgets accessible to screen reader users.

Designing Accessible Widgets

When creating custom widgets or customizing existing ones, consider the following accessibility guidelines:

- **Provide Descriptive Text Alternatives:** Ensure that all visual elements, such as images, icons, and charts, have corresponding text alternatives that convey their meaning and purpose to screen reader users.
- **Use Semantic Markup:** Employ appropriate HTML tags or Qt accessibility roles to define the semantic meaning of your widgets, aiding assistive technologies in understanding their purpose and functionality.
- **Manage Focus Order:** Define a logical tab order for your widgets, allowing keyboard users to navigate through your interface sequentially and predictably.
- **Provide Clear Labels and Instructions:** Use clear and concise labels for input fields, buttons, and other interactive elements. Provide instructions and feedback to guide users through complex tasks.
- **Support Keyboard Shortcuts:** Implement keyboard shortcuts for frequently used

actions, enhancing efficiency and usability for keyboard users.
- **Test with Assistive Technologies:** Regularly test your application with screen readers, magnifiers, and other assistive technologies to identify and address any accessibility barriers.

Accessibility is a vital aspect of modern GUI development, ensuring that your applications are inclusive and usable by individuals with disabilities. Qt's accessibility framework provides a robust foundation for creating accessible interfaces, and by adhering to best practices and leveraging Qt's built-in features, you can craft widgets that cater to the diverse needs of your users.

Chapter 7: QML: Declarative UI Design

Introduction to QML

In the ever-evolving landscape of GUI development, where user expectations for visually stunning and dynamic interfaces continue to soar, Qt introduces QML (Qt Modeling Language), a declarative language that revolutionizes the way you design and build user interfaces. QML empowers you to describe the visual appearance and behavior of your UI in a concise and expressive manner, freeing you from the intricacies of imperative code and enabling rapid prototyping and iteration. In this section, we'll embark on an exploration of QML, unraveling its essence, syntax, and transformative impact on Qt GUI development.

The Essence of QML

QML is a declarative language, meaning you describe *what* you want your UI to look like and *how* it should behave, rather than specifying the step-by-step instructions on *how* to achieve it. This declarative approach shifts the focus from procedural code to a more descriptive and intuitive representation of your UI, fostering clarity, maintainability, and ease of modification.

At its core, QML is built upon JavaScript, a language renowned for its flexibility and dynamic capabilities. This synergy empowers you to leverage JavaScript's expressive syntax and powerful features within the context of UI design, enabling you to create rich and interactive interfaces with remarkable efficiency.

QML's Building Blocks

QML's syntax revolves around the concept of elements, which represent the visual and functional components of your UI. Elements can be nested within each other, forming a hierarchical structure that mirrors the visual composition of your interface.

Each element is defined by its type, properties, and potential child elements. For instance, a `Rectangle` element might have properties for its width, height, color, and border, while a `Text` element might have properties for its text content, font, and alignment.

Properties: Shaping Appearance and Behavior

Properties are the attributes that define the appearance, behavior, and functionality of QML elements. They can be simple values, such as numbers, strings, or colors, or more complex objects, such as animations or transformations.

QML's property binding system allows you to establish dynamic relationships between properties, enabling elements to react and adapt to changes in their environment or user interactions. This reactive programming model fosters the creation of fluid and interactive UIs that respond seamlessly to user input.

Signals and Handlers: Event-Driven Interactions

QML seamlessly integrates with Qt's signal-slot mechanism, enabling you to handle events and user interactions in a declarative manner. Signals, emitted by elements in response to events, can be connected to JavaScript functions, known as handlers, that execute specific actions when the signal is triggered.

This event-driven model empowers you to create responsive and interactive interfaces that react dynamically to user input, such as button clicks, mouse movements, or keyboard events.

Animations and Transitions: Bringing Your UI to Life

QML's animation and transition framework adds a touch of magic to your interfaces, enabling you to create smooth and visually appealing effects that captivate and engage users. You can animate properties of elements, such as position, size, opacity, or color, over time, creating transitions, fades, transformations, and other captivating visual effects.

QML's declarative syntax for animations and transitions simplifies the creation of complex and dynamic behaviors, empowering you to craft UIs that feel alive and responsive.

The Power of QML

QML's declarative nature, JavaScript foundation, and rich feature set make it a powerful tool for Qt GUI development. It offers several key advantages:

- **Rapid Prototyping:** QML's concise syntax and visual design tools enable rapid prototyping and iteration, allowing you to experiment with different UI concepts and refine your design quickly.
- **Separation of Concerns:** QML promotes a clear separation between UI design and application logic, facilitating collaboration between designers and developers.

- **Dynamic and Fluid UIs:** QML's property binding system and animation framework empower you to create modern, touch-friendly interfaces that respond seamlessly to user interactions.
- **Cross-platform Compatibility:** QML-based UIs can be deployed across different platforms, ensuring a consistent user experience across devices.

QML represents a paradigm shift in Qt GUI development, offering a declarative and expressive language for crafting visually stunning and interactive user interfaces. By embracing QML's concepts, syntax, and capabilities, you can unlock a new dimension of creativity and efficiency in your Qt projects.

QML Syntax and Basic Elements

QML's syntax, with its JavaScript-like structure and declarative nature, provides a concise and intuitive way to describe the visual composition and behavior of your user interfaces. In this section, we'll delve into the fundamental elements of QML syntax, exploring its building blocks, property declarations, and basic element types, equipping you with the knowledge to craft your first QML-based UIs.

Elements: The Building Blocks

At the heart of QML syntax lies the concept of elements, which represent the visual and functional components of your UI. Each element is defined by its type, properties, and potential child elements. Elements can be nested within each other, forming a hierarchical structure that mirrors the visual layout of your interface.

QML

```
import QtQuick 2.15

Rectangle {
    width: 200
    height: 100
    color: "blue"

    Text {
        text: "Hello, QML!"
        anchors.centerIn: parent
    }
}
```

In this example, we define a `Rectangle` element with specific width, height, and color properties. Within the `Rectangle`, we nest a `Text` element that displays the text "Hello, QML!". The `anchors.centerIn: parent` property ensures that the `Text` element is centered within its parent `Rectangle`.

Properties: Shaping Appearance and Behavior

Properties are the attributes that define the visual appearance, behavior, and functionality of QML elements. They can be simple values, such as numbers, strings, or colors, or more complex objects, such as animations or transformations.

QML

```
Rectangle {
    id: myRectangle
    width: 200
    height: 100
    color: "green"
    border.width: 2
    border.color: "black"
    radius: 10 // Rounded corners
}
```

In this example, we define a `Rectangle` element with an `id` for reference, specific dimensions, color, border properties, and rounded corners.

Property Binding: Dynamic Relationships

QML's property binding system allows you to establish dynamic relationships between properties, enabling elements to react and adapt to changes in their environment or user interactions. You can bind a property to a JavaScript expression, another property, or even a signal, creating a reactive programming model that fosters the creation of fluid and interactive UIs.

QML

```
Rectangle {
    width: 200
    height: 100
    color: mouseArea.pressed ? "red" : "blue" // Change color on mouse press

    MouseArea {
        id: mouseArea
        anchors.fill: parent
```

```
        }
    }
```

In this example, we bind the `color` property of the `Rectangle` to a JavaScript expression that checks if the `mouseArea` is pressed. If it is, the color changes to red; otherwise, it remains blue.

Basic Element Types

QML offers a rich collection of basic element types that serve as the foundation for building your UIs. Some essential ones include:

- `Item`: The base element type, providing basic positioning and sizing capabilities.
- `Rectangle`: A rectangular visual element, often used as a container or background.
- `Text`: Displays text content with customizable font, color, and alignment.
- `Image`: Displays an image from a file or other source.
- `MouseArea`: An invisible element that captures mouse events, enabling interaction with other elements.

QML's syntax, with its declarative nature, JavaScript foundation, and basic element types, provides a powerful and intuitive way to describe the visual composition and behavior of your user interfaces. By mastering these fundamental concepts, you'll be equipped to craft your first QML-based UIs and embark on a journey of creating dynamic and engaging user experiences.

Integrating QML with C++

While QML shines in its ability to declaratively craft visually captivating and interactive user interfaces, the true power of Qt lies in its seamless integration with C++. This dynamic duo allows you to harness the performance and flexibility of C++ alongside the expressiveness and rapid development capabilities of QML. In this section, we'll delve into the intricacies of integrating QML and C++, exploring techniques that empower you to leverage the strengths of both worlds and build sophisticated GUI applications that push the boundaries of innovation.

The Bridge Between Two Worlds

Qt's meta-object system serves as the bridge between QML and C++, enabling seamless communication and interaction between the two. This integration allows QML to access properties, methods, and signals of any `QObject`-derived C++ class, effectively extending the QML environment with the full power and capabilities of your C++ code.

Exposing C++ Functionality to QML

To expose C++ functionality to QML, you employ a combination of Qt's meta-object system and QML's import mechanism. Let's explore the key techniques:

1. **Registering C++ Types:** Use the `qmlRegisterType()` function to register your C++ classes as QML types. This makes your classes available for instantiation and use within QML code.

C++

```
qmlRegisterType<MyClass>("com.mycompany.mymodule", 1, 0, "MyClass");
```

In this example, we register the `MyClass` C++ class as a QML type under the module `com.mycompany.mymodule` with version 1.0.

2. **Exposing Properties, Methods, and Signals:** Decorate your C++ class members with the `Q_PROPERTY`, `Q_INVOKABLE`, and `signals` macros to expose them to QML. Properties can be read and modified from QML, methods can be invoked from QML expressions, and signal handlers are automatically created for signals.

C++

```
class MyClass : public QObject
{
    Q_OBJECT
        Q_PROPERTY(int myProperty READ myProperty WRITE setMyProperty NOTIFY myPropertyChanged)

public:
    explicit MyClass(QObject *parent = nullptr);

    int myProperty() const;
        void    setMyProperty(int newProperty);
```

```
signals:
    void myPropertyChanged();

private:
    int m_myProperty;
};
```

In this example, we expose the `myProperty` member variable as a QML property, allowing it to be accessed and modified from QML. We also expose a signal `myPropertyChanged` to notify QML about property changes.

3. **Importing C++ Modules:** Use the `import` statement in your QML code to import the registered C++ modules and access their types.

QML

```
import QtQuick 2.15
import com.mycompany.mymodule 1.0

MyClass {
```

```
    myProperty: 42
}
```

In this QML snippet, we import the `com.mycompany.mymodule` module and instantiate a `MyClass` object, setting its `myProperty` to 42.

Embedding C++ Objects into QML

Qt also allows you to embed C++ objects directly into the context of QML components using context properties. This enables you to inject data or functionality from C++ into QML, facilitating seamless integration and communication between the two.

C++

```
QQmlApplicationEngine engine;
MyClass* myObject = new MyClass;
engine.rootContext()->setContextProperty("myObject", myObject);
engine.load(QUrl(QStringLiteral("qrc:/main.qml")));
```

In this C++ code, we create a `MyClass` object and set it as a context property named `myObject`. This makes the `myObject` accessible within the QML environment.

QML

```
import QtQuick 2.15

Text {
    text: myObject.myProperty
}
```

In this QML snippet, we access the `myProperty` of the `myObject` context property, effectively retrieving data from the embedded C++ object.

Best Practices

To ensure a smooth and effective integration between QML and C++, adhere to the following best practices:

- **Keep QML declarative:** Strive to keep your QML code declarative, focusing on describing the UI's structure and behavior rather than implementing complex logic.
- **Delegate complex logic to C++:** Use C++ for computationally intensive tasks, data processing, or algorithms that require fine-grained control or performance optimizations.
- **Minimize data transfer between QML and C++:** Avoid excessive data marshaling between QML and C++ to maintain performance and responsiveness.
- **Use signals and slots for communication:** Leverage Qt's signal-slot mechanism to facilitate communication between QML and C++ components.
- **Test thoroughly:** Rigorously test your QML and C++ integration to ensure seamless interaction and error-free behavior.

Integrating QML with C++ unlocks the full potential of Qt, allowing you to harness the performance and flexibility of C++ alongside the expressiveness and rapid development capabilities of QML. By mastering the techniques for exposing C++ functionality to QML and embedding C++ objects into the QML context, you can build sophisticated

GUI applications that seamlessly blend the strengths of both worlds.

Building Dynamic UIs with QML

In the realm of modern GUI development, static and rigid interfaces are a relic of the past. Today's users demand dynamic and responsive UIs that adapt seamlessly to their interactions and data changes. QML, with its declarative nature, property binding system, and JavaScript expressions, empowers you to craft such dynamic interfaces with remarkable ease and elegance. In this section, we'll embark on a journey to explore the techniques for building dynamic UIs with QML, unlocking the potential to create interfaces that feel alive, interactive, and engaging.

Property Binding: The Engine of Dynamism

At the heart of QML's dynamic capabilities lies its property binding system. Property bindings establish dynamic relationships between properties, enabling elements to react and adapt to changes in their environment or user interactions. This reactive programming model fosters the creation of UIs that respond fluidly and intuitively to user input, data updates, and other events.

QML

```
import QtQuick 2.15

Rectangle {
    width: 200
    height: 100
    color: slider.value > 50 ? "green" : "red"

    Slider {
        id: slider
        from: 0
        to: 100
    }
}
```

In this example, the `color` property of the `Rectangle` is bound to a JavaScript expression that evaluates the value of the `slider`. If the slider's value is greater than 50, the rectangle turns green; otherwise, it remains red. As the user interacts with the slider, the rectangle's color dynamically changes, reflecting the updated value.

JavaScript Expressions: Unleashing Flexibility

QML seamlessly integrates JavaScript expressions into its property bindings, granting you the flexibility to perform calculations, manipulate data, and define complex conditional logic directly within your UI declarations.

QML

```
import QtQuick 2.15

Text {
    text: "The sum of 3 and 5 is " + (3 + 5)
}
```

In this snippet, we use a JavaScript expression within the `text` property of a `Text` element to calculate and display the sum of 3 and 5. This demonstrates how QML empowers you to embed logic directly within your UI, promoting a concise and expressive representation of your interface's behavior.

Conditional Rendering: Adapting to Context

QML's conditional rendering capabilities allow you to dynamically show or hide elements based on specific conditions or data states. This enables you to create UIs that adapt to different contexts, user preferences, or application logic.

QML

```
import QtQuick 2.15

Item {
    property bool isLoggedIn: false

    Text {
        text: "Welcome, user!"
        visible: isLoggedIn
    }

    Button {
        text: "Login"
        visible: !isLoggedIn
        onClicked: isLoggedIn = true
    }
}
```

In this example, we define a `isLoggedIn` property and conditionally render a welcome message or a login button based on its value. When the user clicks the login button, the `isLoggedIn` property is set to `true`, triggering a UI update that hides the button and displays the welcome message.

Lists and Models: Dynamic Data Presentation

QML provides powerful tools for dynamically presenting and interacting with data through lists and models. The `ListView` element, coupled with data models like `ListModel` or `XmlListModel`, allows you to create scrollable lists that efficiently display and update data from various sources.

QML

```
import QtQuick 2.15

ListView {
    model: ListModel {
        ListElement { name: "Alice" }
        ListElement { name: "Bob" }
        ListElement { name: "Charlie"
}
    }

    delegate: Text { text: name }
```

}

In this example, we create a `ListView` that displays a list of names from a `ListModel`. The `delegate` property defines how each list item is rendered, in this case using a `Text` element to display the `name` property of each `ListElement`.

QML's declarative nature, property binding system, JavaScript expressions, and conditional rendering capabilities empower you to build dynamic UIs that respond seamlessly to user interactions and data changes. By mastering these techniques, you can create interfaces that feel alive, interactive, and engaging, delivering exceptional user experiences across a variety of devices and screen sizes.

Part III: Advanced Qt Techniques

Chapter 8: Model-View Architecture: Structuring Your Data

Understanding the Model-View Paradigm

In the realm of GUI development, where data presentation and manipulation are paramount, the Model-View paradigm emerges as a guiding principle for structuring and organizing your application's data. Qt's implementation of this paradigm, known as the Model-View architecture, provides a powerful and flexible framework for decoupling data storage, data presentation, and user interaction. In this section, we'll embark on a journey to unravel the essence of the Model-View paradigm, exploring its core components, benefits, and practical applications in crafting robust and maintainable Qt GUI applications.

The Triad of Model, View, and Delegate

At the heart of the Model-View architecture lies a triad of interconnected components:

1. **Model**: The model represents the underlying data structure, encapsulating the storage and management of your application's data. It acts as a source of information, providing

data to views for presentation and responding to data modification requests.
2. **View**: The view is responsible for presenting the data provided by the model to the user in a visually meaningful way. It renders the data, handles user interactions, and communicates any changes back to the model.
3. **Delegate**: The delegate acts as a bridge between the model and the view, controlling the rendering and editing of individual data items within the view. It provides a customizable way to display and interact with each data element, offering flexibility and fine-grained control over the presentation.

Decoupling for Flexibility

The Model-View architecture's strength lies in its decoupling of data storage, presentation, and interaction. This separation of concerns offers several key benefits:

- **Data Independence**: The model is independent of the views that display its data. This allows you to change the presentation of your data without affecting

the underlying data structure or the code that manipulates it.
- **Multiple Views**: A single model can be connected to multiple views, each presenting the data in a different way. This enables you to create diverse and flexible user interfaces that cater to different user needs or contexts.
- **Customizability**: Delegates provide a customizable way to render and edit individual data items within a view. This allows you to tailor the presentation and interaction of each element to your specific requirements.
- **Maintainability**: The separation of concerns promotes cleaner and more maintainable code. Changes to the model, view, or delegate can be made independently without affecting the other components, facilitating easier debugging and updates.

Qt's Model-View Classes

Qt provides a rich collection of classes that implement the Model-View architecture:

- **Models**: Qt offers several built-in model classes, including `QStringListModel`, `QStandardItemModel`, and

`QSqlQueryModel`, each catering to different data structures and sources. You can also create custom models by subclassing `QAbstractItemModel` or one of its convenience subclasses.
- **Views**: Qt provides various view classes, such as `QListView`, `QTableView`, and `QTreeView`, each designed to present data in a specific way. These views automatically connect to models and handle the rendering and interaction with the data.
- **Delegates**: Qt's default delegate, `QStyledItemDelegate`, provides basic rendering and editing capabilities for most data types. You can also create custom delegates by subclassing `QStyledItemDelegate` or `QAbstractItemDelegate` to achieve specialized presentation and interaction.

The Flow of Data

In the Model-View architecture, data flows seamlessly between the model, view, and delegate:

1. The view requests data from the model.
2. The model provides the requested data to the view.

3. The view uses the delegate to render and display each data item.
4. The user interacts with the view, potentially modifying the data.
5. The view communicates any data changes back to the model.
6. The model updates its internal data structure and notifies any connected views about the changes.
7. The views refresh their display to reflect the updated data.

The Model-View paradigm, implemented through Qt's Model-View architecture, provides a powerful and flexible framework for structuring and organizing your application's data. By decoupling data storage, presentation, and interaction, it promotes data independence, multiple views, customizability, and maintainability.

Built-in Qt Models

Qt's Model-View architecture comes equipped with a collection of built-in model classes that cater to a variety of common data structures and sources. These pre-built models provide convenient and efficient ways to represent and manage data within your Qt applications, eliminating the need to create custom models from scratch in many scenarios. In this section, we'll explore some of the essential built-in Qt models, highlighting their characteristics, use cases, and practical applications in GUI development.

QStringListModel: Simplicity for String Lists

The `QStringListModel` class is a straightforward model designed specifically for handling lists of strings. It provides a simple and intuitive interface for storing, accessing, and modifying string data. `QStringListModel` is ideal for scenarios where you need to display a list of options, such as a dropdown menu or a list of selectable items.

C++

```
QStringListModel* model = new QStringListModel(this);
QStringList list;
list << "Apple" << "Banana" << "Orange";
model->setStringList(list);

QListView* view = new QListView(this);
view->setModel(model);
```

In this example, we create a `QStringListModel` and populate it with a list of fruits. We then connect the model to a `QListView`, which automatically renders the list of fruits for the user.

QStandardItemModel: Versatility for Item-Based Data

The `QStandardItemModel` class offers a more versatile approach to data representation, handling item-based data organized in a hierarchical structure. It allows you to create tables, trees, or lists with customizable headers, rows, and columns. `QStandardItemModel` is suitable for scenarios where you need to display and manipulate structured data, such as spreadsheets, file explorers, or hierarchical navigation menus.

C++

```
QStandardItemModel* model = new QStandardItemModel(this);
model->setHorizontalHeaderLabels(QStringList() << "Name" << "Age");

QList<QStandardItem*> rowItems;
rowItems << new QStandardItem("Alice") << new QStandardItem("25");
model->appendRow(rowItems);
```

```
rowItems.clear();
rowItems << new QStandardItem("Bob")
<< new QStandardItem("30");
model->appendRow(rowItems);

QTableView*      view      =      new
QTableView(this);
view->setModel(model);
```

In this example, we create a `QStandardItemModel` with two columns: "Name" and "Age." We then populate the model with two rows of data, representing individuals and their ages. Finally, we connect the model to a `QTableView`, which renders the data in a tabular format.

QSqlQueryModel: Bridging the Gap to Databases

The `QSqlQueryModel` class acts as a bridge between your Qt application and a database, enabling you to execute SQL queries and display the resulting data in views like `QTableView`. It simplifies the process of retrieving and presenting database information, making it an invaluable tool for database-driven applications.

C++

```
QSqlDatabase db = QSqlDatabase::addDatabase("QSQLITE");
db.setDatabaseName("mydatabase.db");
db.open();

QSqlQueryModel* model = new QSqlQueryModel(this);
model->setQuery("SELECT name, age FROM users");

QTableView* view = new QTableView(this);
view->setModel(model);
```

In this example, we establish a connection to an SQLite database and execute a query to retrieve the "name" and "age" columns from the "users" table. We then create a `QSqlQueryModel` and set its query, automatically populating the model with the query results. Finally, we connect the model to a `QTableView`, which displays the retrieved data in a tabular format.

Choosing the Right Model

Selecting the appropriate built-in model depends on the nature of your data and the desired presentation. Consider the following factors:

- **Data Structure:** Is your data a simple list of strings, a hierarchical structure of items, or information stored in a database?
- **Data Source:** Is your data static or dynamic? Does it originate from a file, a database, or another source?
- **View Type:** What type of view will you be using to present the data (e.g., list, table, tree)?
- **Customization Needs:** Do you require fine-grained control over the rendering and editing of individual data items?

By carefully evaluating these factors, you can choose the built-in model that best suits your requirements, streamlining your development process and ensuring efficient data handling within your Qt applications.

Qt's built-in models provide a convenient and efficient way to represent and manage data within your GUI applications. By understanding their characteristics, use cases, and limitations, you can leverage these pre-built models to accelerate development and create user interfaces that seamlessly interact with your data.

Creating Custom Models

While Qt's built-in models offer convenience for handling common data structures, there are scenarios where your application's data demands a more tailored and specialized approach. In such cases, Qt empowers you to create custom models, granting you the flexibility to represent and manage complex data structures, implement custom logic, and fine-tune the presentation of your data within views. In this section, we'll delve into the art of crafting custom models, exploring the key classes, concepts, and techniques involved in building these bespoke data representations.

Subclassing QAbstractItemModel

At the heart of custom model creation lies the `QAbstractItemModel` class, an abstract base class that defines the interface for all Qt models. By subclassing `QAbstractItemModel`, you inherit its core functionalities and provide your own implementations for its virtual functions, tailoring the model's behavior to your specific data structure and requirements.

C++

```cpp
class MyCustomModel : public QAbstractItemModel
{
    Q_OBJECT

public:
    explicit MyCustomModel(QObject *parent = nullptr);
    ~MyCustomModel();

    // Implement virtual functions from QAbstractItemModel
    QModelIndex index(int row, int column, const QModelIndex &parent = QModelIndex()) const override;
    QModelIndex parent(const QModelIndex &index) const override;
    int rowCount(const QModelIndex &parent = QModelIndex()) const override;
```

```cpp
    int columnCount(const QModelIndex &parent = QModelIndex()) const override;
    QVariant data(const QModelIndex &index, int role = Qt::DisplayRole) const override;
    // ... other virtual functions ...

private:
    // Data storage and other private members
};
```

In this example, we define a custom model class `MyCustomModel` that inherits from `QAbstractItemModel`. We override essential virtual functions like `index()`, `parent()`, `rowCount()`, `columnCount()`, and `data()`, providing implementations that reflect our custom data structure and logic.

Key Virtual Functions

Let's explore some of the key virtual functions you'll typically override when creating custom models:

- `index()`: Returns the model index associated with a given row, column, and parent index. This function is crucial for navigating the data hierarchy and accessing individual data items.
- `parent()`: Returns the parent index of a given model index. This function establishes the hierarchical relationships between data items within the model.
- `rowCount()` and `columnCount()`: Return the number of rows and columns, respectively, in the model or a specific branch of the data hierarchy.
- `data()`: Retrieves the data associated with a given model index and role. Roles define the type of data being requested, such as display text, edit data, or decoration.
- `setData()`: Sets the data for a given model index and role, enabling data modification and updates.
- `flags()`: Returns flags indicating the capabilities of a given model index, such as whether it's editable, selectable, or checkable.
- `headerData()`: Provides data for the headers of the model, such as column or row labels.

Data Storage and Management

Within your custom model, you'll need to implement the data storage and management mechanisms that align with your specific data structure. This might involve using standard library containers like `std::vector` or `std::map`, custom data structures, or even external data sources like databases or files.

Ensure that your model provides efficient access to data, supports data modification and updates, and emits appropriate signals to notify connected views about any changes.

Example: A Custom Tree Model

Let's illustrate the creation of a custom tree model that represents a file system hierarchy:

C++

```
class FileSystemModel : public QAbstractItemModel
{
    // ... implementation ...

private:
    QDir rootDir;
    // ... other private members ...
```

```
};
```

In this example, we define a custom model `FileSystemModel` that uses a `QDir` object to represent the root directory of the file system. The model's virtual functions would then be implemented to traverse the file system hierarchy, retrieve file and directory information, and handle user interactions like expanding or collapsing directories.

Creating custom models empowers you to represent and manage complex data structures, implement custom logic, and fine-tune the presentation of your data within Qt views. By subclassing `QAbstractItemModel` and overriding its key virtual functions, you gain the flexibility to tailor your models to your application's specific requirements.

Data Visualization with Views

In the realm of Qt GUI development, the presentation of data is paramount. Raw data, while valuable, often lacks the visual clarity and accessibility necessary for effective communication and user engagement. Qt's Model-View architecture bridges this gap, offering a powerful framework for seamlessly connecting data models to views, enabling the visualization and interaction with data in a visually compelling and intuitive manner. In this section, we'll embark on a journey to explore the art of data visualization with Qt views, unraveling their capabilities, customization options, and practical applications in crafting informative and engaging user interfaces.

Qt's View Classes: A Visual Feast

Qt provides a rich collection of view classes, each tailored to present data in a specific way, catering to diverse visualization needs. Let's explore some of the essential view classes and their applications:

- `QListView`: Presents data as a list of items, ideal for displaying collections of text, images, or other elements. It supports various layouts, including vertical, horizontal, and grid layouts, and allows for customization of item delegates to control the visual representation of each item.
- `QTableView`: Renders data in a tabular format with rows and columns, resembling a spreadsheet. It excels in presenting

structured data with clear relationships between columns and rows. `QTableView` supports sorting, filtering, and editing, empowering users to interact with and manipulate the data directly within the view.
- `QTreeView`: Displays hierarchical data in a tree-like structure with expandable and collapsible branches. It's perfect for visualizing file systems, organizational charts, or any data with parent-child relationships. `QTreeView` enables users to navigate through the data hierarchy and interact with individual items at different levels.
- `QColumnView`: Presents data in columns, where each column represents a specific attribute or category. It's suitable for browsing and filtering large datasets based on columnar criteria.
- `QListWidget` **and** `QTreeWidget`: Convenience classes that provide item-based lists and trees, respectively. They offer a simpler interface compared to their model-based counterparts but sacrifice some flexibility in data handling and customization.

Connecting Models and Views

The magic of Qt's Model-View architecture lies in its ability to seamlessly connect data models to views. Once you have a model representing your data, you can associate it with a view using the `setModel()` function. The view will then automatically retrieve data from the model and render it according to its specific presentation style.

C++

```
QStandardItemModel* model = new QStandardItemModel(this);
// Populate the model with data

QTableView* view = new QTableView(this);
view->setModel(model);
```

In this example, we create a `QStandardItemModel` and populate it with data. We then connect the model to a `QTableView`, which renders the data in a tabular format.

Customizing Views with Delegates

Delegates play a crucial role in customizing the visual representation and interaction of individual data items within a view. Qt's default delegate, `QStyledItemDelegate`, provides basic rendering and editing capabilities for most data types. However, you can create custom delegates by subclassing `QStyledItemDelegate` or `QAbstractItemDelegate` to achieve specialized presentation and behavior.

C++

```
class MyCustomDelegate : public QStyledItemDelegate
{
    Q_OBJECT

public:
    explicit MyCustomDelegate(QObject *parent = nullptr);

    void paint(QPainter *painter, const QStyleOptionViewItem &option, const QModelIndex &index) const override;
    QSize sizeHint(const QStyleOptionViewItem &option, const QModelIndex &index) const override;
    // ... other virtual functions ...
```

```
};
```

In this example, we define a custom delegate `MyCustomDelegate` that inherits from `QStyledItemDelegate`. We override the `paint()` function to customize the visual rendering of each item and the `sizeHint()` function to provide size hints for the items.

Interactive Data Visualization

Qt views not only present data visually but also enable user interaction and manipulation. Depending on the view type and its configuration, users can:

- **Select items:** Highlight individual or multiple items within the view.
- **Edit data:** Modify the values of data items directly within the view.
- **Sort and filter data:** Rearrange or narrow down the displayed data based on specific criteria.
- **Drag and drop items:** Move items within the view or between different views.

These interactive features empower users to explore, analyze, and modify data in a dynamic and intuitive manner, enhancing the overall user experience.

Qt's Model-View architecture, coupled with its rich collection of view classes and customizable delegates, provides a powerful framework for visualizing and interacting with data in your GUI applications. By harnessing the capabilities of Qt views, you can transform raw data into informative and engaging visual representations, empowering users to explore, analyze, and manipulate information with ease.

Chapter 9: Database Integration: Connecting to Your Data

Qt SQL Module

In the realm of modern applications, data persistence and retrieval are paramount. The ability to seamlessly interact with databases empowers your Qt applications to store, manage, and retrieve information efficiently, fostering a dynamic and data-driven user experience. Qt's SQL module emerges as the bridge between your application and the world of databases, providing a comprehensive set of classes and functions that streamline database integration and simplify data access. In this section, we'll embark on an exploration of the Qt SQL module, unraveling its capabilities, key classes, and practical applications in connecting your Qt GUIs to the underlying data that fuels them.

The Essence of the Qt SQL Module

The Qt SQL module acts as a powerful intermediary between your Qt application and various database systems. It abstracts the underlying database-specific complexities, providing a unified and platform-independent interface for interacting with databases. This abstraction empowers you to write code that is portable across different database backends, such as SQLite, PostgreSQL, MySQL, and Oracle, without requiring significant modifications.

Key Classes and Functionalities

The Qt SQL module encompasses a collection of classes and functions that facilitate database integration. Let's explore some of the key players:

- `QSqlDatabase`: Represents a connection to a database. It encapsulates the connection parameters, such as the database driver, hostname, database name, username, and password.
- `QSqlQuery`: Executes SQL queries against a database and retrieves the resulting data. It provides methods for preparing and executing queries, binding values to placeholders, and iterating over the result set.
- `QSqlTableModel`: A versatile model class that seamlessly integrates with Qt's Model-View architecture. It represents a table in a database, enabling you to display and manipulate database data directly within Qt views like `QTableView`.

- `QSqlQueryModel`: A model class that executes a single SQL query and presents the resulting data in a read-only fashion. It's ideal for scenarios where you need to display the output of a query without requiring data modification capabilities.
- `QSqlRelationalTableModel`: Extends `QSqlTableModel` to handle relationships between tables in a database. It simplifies the management of foreign key constraints and provides convenient access to related data.

Database Drivers: Connecting the Dots

To establish a connection between your Qt application and a specific database backend, you'll need the corresponding database driver. Qt supports a wide range of database drivers, including:

- **QSQLITE**: For the lightweight and embedded SQLite database.
- **QPSQL**: For the powerful and open-source PostgreSQL database.
- **QMYSQL**: For the popular MySQL database.
- **QOCI**: For the Oracle database.

Ensure that you have the appropriate driver installed and configured on your system before attempting to connect to a database.

SQL Abstraction: A Unified Language

Qt's SQL module employs SQL (Structured Query Language) as the common language for interacting with databases. SQL provides a standardized way to define, query, and manipulate data, regardless of the underlying database backend. This abstraction empowers you to write SQL queries that are portable across different database systems, enhancing the flexibility and maintainability of your code.

Error Handling and Transactions

The Qt SQL module provides robust error handling mechanisms to gracefully manage database-related errors. The `QSqlError` class encapsulates error information, including the error code, driver text, and database text. You can use this information to diagnose and resolve issues during database operations.

Furthermore, Qt supports transactions, allowing you to group multiple SQL statements into a single unit of work. This ensures data integrity and consistency, as all statements within a transaction are either executed successfully or rolled back entirely in case of an error.

Beyond the Basics

The Qt SQL module offers additional features and capabilities beyond the core classes and functionalities mentioned above. These include:

- **Prepared Queries**: Enhance performance and security by precompiling SQL queries and binding values to placeholders at runtime.
- **BLOB Support**: Store and retrieve binary large objects (BLOBs), such as images or documents, within your database.
- **Database Metadata**: Access information about database tables, columns, and other schema elements.
- **Custom SQL Dialects**: Extend Qt's SQL support to handle database-specific syntax or features.

Qt's SQL module serves as a powerful conduit between your Qt applications and the world of databases. By abstracting database-specific complexities and providing a unified interface, it empowers you to seamlessly integrate database interactions into your GUIs, fostering dynamic and data-driven user experiences.

Connecting to Databases

Establishing a connection between your Qt application and a database is the first step towards harnessing the power of data persistence and retrieval. Qt's SQL module provides a straightforward and flexible mechanism for connecting to various database backends, empowering you to seamlessly integrate your GUI with the underlying data that fuels it. In this section, we'll delve into the intricacies of database connections in Qt, exploring the necessary steps, configuration options, and best practices for establishing robust and secure connections.

Choosing the Right Database Driver

Qt's SQL module supports a wide range of database drivers, each catering to a specific database backend. Before establishing a connection, ensure that you have the appropriate driver installed and configured on your system. Some common database drivers include:

- **QSQLITE**: For the lightweight and embedded SQLite database.

- **QPSQL**: For the powerful and open-source PostgreSQL database.
- **QMYSQL**: For the popular MySQL database.
- **QOCI**: For the Oracle database.

You can obtain the necessary drivers from the Qt website or through your operating system's package manager. Once installed, make sure the drivers are accessible to your Qt application by configuring the appropriate environment variables or library paths.

Establishing the Connection

Qt's `QSqlDatabase` class represents a connection to a database. To establish a connection, you first need to create a `QSqlDatabase` object and specify the connection parameters, such as the database driver, hostname, database name, username, and password.

C++

```
QSqlDatabase db = QSqlDatabase::addDatabase("QSQLITE");
db.setDatabaseName("mydatabase.db");

if (!db.open()) {
```

```
        qDebug() << "Error: connection
with database failed";
} else {
      qDebug() << "Database: connection
ok";
}
```

In this example, we create a `QSqlDatabase` object and set the database driver to "QSQLITE." We then specify the database name as "mydatabase.db." Finally, we attempt to open the connection using the `open()` function. If the connection is successful, we print a success message; otherwise, we display an error message.

Connection Parameters

The specific connection parameters required depend on the database backend you're connecting to. Here's a general overview of common parameters:

- **Driver**: The name of the database driver (e.g., "QSQLITE," "QPSQL," "QMYSQL," "QOCI").

- **Hostname**: The hostname or IP address of the database server. For embedded databases like SQLite, this might be an empty string or a file path.
- **Database Name**: The name of the database to connect to.
- **Username**: The username for authentication.
- **Password**: The password for authentication.
- **Port**: The port number on which the database server is listening.

Consult the Qt documentation for the specific driver you're using to obtain the complete list of supported connection parameters and their default values.

Connection Management

Qt allows you to manage multiple database connections simultaneously within your application. Each connection is identified by a unique connection name. You can use the `QSqlDatabase::addDatabase()` function to create new connections and the `QSqlDatabase::database()` function to retrieve existing connections by their name.

C++

```cpp
QSqlDatabase db1 = QSqlDatabase::addDatabase("QPSQL", "connection1");
// Set connection parameters for db1

QSqlDatabase db2 = QSqlDatabase::addDatabase("QMYSQL", "connection2");
// Set connection parameters for db2

// ... use db1 and db2 ...

db1.close();
db2.close();
```

In this example, we create two database connections, one to a PostgreSQL database and another to a MySQL database. We assign unique connection names to each connection, allowing us to manage and access them independently.

Best Practices

To ensure robust and secure database connections, adhere to the following best practices:

- **Validate Input**: Sanitize and validate user input before incorporating it into SQL queries to prevent SQL injection vulnerabilities.
- **Use Prepared Queries**: Employ prepared queries to enhance performance and security by precompiling SQL statements and binding values to placeholders at runtime.
- **Handle Errors Gracefully**: Implement error handling mechanisms to catch and manage database-related errors, providing informative feedback to the user.
- **Close Connections When Done**: Explicitly close database connections when they are no longer needed to release resources and avoid potential conflicts.
- **Consider Connection Pooling**: For performance-critical applications, explore connection pooling techniques to reuse existing connections and reduce the overhead of establishing new ones.

Connecting to databases is a fundamental step in integrating your Qt applications with the data that drives them. By understanding the process of selecting drivers, configuring connection parameters, and managing multiple connections, you can establish robust and secure links between your GUI and the underlying data sources.

Executing Queries and Retrieving Data

Once you've established a connection to your database, the next step in harnessing the power of data persistence is to execute SQL queries and retrieve the resulting information. Qt's SQL module provides a flexible and intuitive mechanism for interacting with your database, empowering you to extract, manipulate, and update data with precision and efficiency. In this section, we'll delve into the art of executing queries and retrieving data in Qt, exploring the key classes, techniques, and best practices for seamlessly interacting with your database.

The QSqlQuery Class: Your SQL Maestro

The `QSqlQuery` class serves as your SQL maestro, orchestrating the execution of queries against your database and managing the retrieval of the resulting data. It provides a comprehensive set of methods for preparing, executing, and navigating through query results, empowering you to interact with your database in a structured and controlled manner.

Preparing and Executing Queries

To execute a SQL query, you first need to create a `QSqlQuery` object and associate it with an open database connection. You can then use the `prepare()` method to prepare your SQL statement, replacing any dynamic values with placeholders. Finally, you invoke the `exec()` method to execute the prepared query against the database.

C++

```
QSqlQuery query(db); // Assuming 'db' is an open QSqlDatabase connection

query.prepare("SELECT name, age FROM users WHERE age > :age_limit");
query.bindValue(":age_limit", 25);

if (query.exec()) {
    while (query.next()) {
        QString name = query.value("name").toString();
        int age = query.value("age").toInt();
        qDebug() << name << "is" << age << "years old.";
    }
}
```

```
} else {
    qDebug() << "Query failed:" << query.lastError().text();
}
```

In this example, we prepare a SQL query to select the "name" and "age" columns from the "users" table, filtering by an age limit specified through a placeholder. We then bind the value 25 to the placeholder using `bindValue()`. Finally, we execute the query and iterate over the result set using `next()`, retrieving and printing the values of each row.

Binding Values: Enhancing Security and Performance

Binding values to placeholders in prepared queries offers several advantages:

- **Security**: It helps prevent SQL injection attacks by separating SQL code from user-supplied data.
- **Performance**: Prepared queries can be precompiled by the database server, leading

to faster execution times, especially for frequently executed queries.
- **Readability**: It improves code readability by clearly separating SQL code from dynamic values.

Qt provides various methods for binding values to placeholders, including `bindValue()`, `addBindValue()`, and `boundValues()`. Choose the appropriate method based on your specific query and data types.

Navigating the Result Set

Once a query is executed successfully, you can navigate through the result set using the `next()` method. This method advances the query to the next row in the result set and returns `true` if a valid row is available; otherwise, it returns `false`.

You can then retrieve the values of each column in the current row using the `value()` method, specifying the column name or index. Qt automatically converts the retrieved values to appropriate QVariant objects, which can be further converted to specific data types using methods like `toString()`, `toInt()`, or `toDouble()`.

Handling Query Errors

Database operations are susceptible to errors, such as invalid queries, connection issues, or data integrity violations. Qt's SQL module provides robust error handling mechanisms to gracefully manage such errors. The `QSqlError` class encapsulates error information, including the error code, driver text, and database text. You can use this information to diagnose and resolve issues during query execution.

C++

```
if (!query.exec()) {
            QSqlError error = query.lastError();
      qDebug() << "Query error:" << error.text();
    // Handle the error appropriately
}
```

In this example, we check the return value of the `exec()` method to determine if the query execution was successful. If an error occurs, we retrieve the error information using `lastError()` and handle it accordingly, potentially displaying an error message to the user or logging the error for debugging purposes.

Conclusion

Executing SQL queries and retrieving data are fundamental operations in database integration. Qt's SQL module, with its `QSqlQuery` class and associated methods, provides a flexible and intuitive mechanism for interacting with your database. By mastering the techniques for preparing, executing, and navigating through query results, you can seamlessly extract, manipulate, and update data, empowering your Qt applications to become truly data-driven.

Displaying Data in Your GUI

The ability to seamlessly integrate data from your database into your Qt GUI is the final piece of the puzzle in creating dynamic and data-driven applications. Qt's Model-View architecture provides an elegant solution, enabling you to connect your database query results to views like `QTableView`, `QListView`, or `QTreeView`, effortlessly transforming raw data into visually compelling and interactive representations. In this section, we'll explore the techniques and best practices for displaying data in your Qt GUI, empowering you to craft user interfaces that inform, engage, and empower your users.

Leveraging Qt's Model-View Architecture

Qt's Model-View architecture serves as the conduit between your data and its visual representation. The model encapsulates the data retrieved from your database, while the view renders this data in a user-friendly format. This decoupling of data and presentation offers flexibility, maintainability, and the ability to present the same data in multiple views simultaneously.

QSqlTableModel: The Table Maestro

The `QSqlTableModel` class is a powerful tool for displaying database tables within your GUI. It acts as a bridge between your database table and a `QTableView`, automatically handling data retrieval, presentation, and even editing capabilities.

C++

```
QSqlTableModel* model = new QSqlTableModel(this);
model->setTable("users");
model->select();
```

```cpp
QTableView* view = new QTableView(this);
view->setModel(model);
```

In this example, we create a `QSqlTableModel` and associate it with the "users" table in our database. The `select()` method retrieves the data from the table and populates the model. We then connect the model to a `QTableView`, which renders the table data in a user-friendly grid format, complete with column headers and row selection.

QSqlQueryModel: Read-Only Presentation

The `QSqlQueryModel` class offers a read-only view of your database query results. It's ideal for scenarios where you need to display the output of a query without requiring data modification capabilities.

C++

```cpp
QSqlQueryModel* model = new QSqlQueryModel(this);
```

```cpp
model->setQuery("SELECT name, age FROM users WHERE age > 25");

QListView* view = new QListView(this);
view->setModel(model);
```

In this example, we create a `QSqlQueryModel` and set its query to retrieve the "name" and "age" columns from the "users" table, filtering by an age limit. We then connect the model to a `QListView`, which displays the query results as a list of items.

Custom Delegates: Tailored Presentation

While Qt's default delegate provides basic rendering and editing capabilities, you can create custom delegates to achieve specialized presentation and interaction for your data items. This empowers you to control the visual appearance, formatting, and behavior of each item within the view.

C++

```cpp
class MyCustomDelegate : public QStyledItemDelegate
```

```
{
    // ... implementation ...
};

QTableView* view = new QTableView(this);
view->setItemDelegate(new MyCustomDelegate(this));
```

In this example, we create a custom delegate `MyCustomDelegate` and set it as the item delegate for a `QTableView`. This allows us to customize the rendering and editing of individual cells within the table, tailoring the presentation to our specific needs.

Beyond Tables and Lists

Qt's Model-View architecture extends beyond tables and lists, offering views for various data visualization scenarios:

- `QTreeView`: Ideal for displaying hierarchical data, such as file systems or organizational charts.

- `QColumnView`: Suitable for browsing and filtering large datasets based on columnar criteria.
- **Custom Views**: You can create custom views by subclassing `QAbstractItemView` to achieve unique data presentation and interaction paradigms.

Best Practices

To ensure effective and maintainable data visualization in your Qt GUIs, adhere to the following best practices:

- **Choose the Right View**: Select the view class that best aligns with the nature of your data and the desired presentation style.
- **Leverage Models**: Utilize Qt's built-in models or create custom models to encapsulate your data and provide a clean interface for views.
- **Customize with Delegates**: Employ custom delegates to tailor the visual representation and interaction of individual data items.
- **Handle Data Changes Gracefully**: Implement mechanisms to update views whenever the underlying data changes, ensuring a consistent and up-to-date presentation.

- **Consider Performance**: Optimize your data handling and rendering to ensure smooth and responsive performance, especially when dealing with large datasets.

Displaying data in your Qt GUI is a crucial aspect of creating informative and engaging applications. Qt's Model-View architecture, coupled with its diverse collection of view classes and customizable delegates, empowers you to seamlessly integrate data from your database into your interfaces, transforming raw information into visually compelling and interactive representations.

Chapter 10: Networking: Communicating with the World

Qt Network Module

In the interconnected digital landscape of today, where applications often transcend the boundaries of a single device, the ability to communicate seamlessly over networks is paramount. Qt's Network module emerges as the enabler of this connectivity, equipping your applications with the tools and capabilities to interact with the vast expanse of the internet and other networked resources. In this section, we will embark on an exploration of the Qt Network module, unraveling its core components, functionalities, and practical applications in building networked Qt applications that thrive in the digital age.

The Essence of the Qt Network Module

The Qt Network module serves as a comprehensive toolkit for network programming in Qt, providing a high-level and platform-independent interface for various network protocols and operations. It abstracts the underlying complexities of network communication, empowering you to focus on the core logic of your applications without getting bogged down in low-level details.

Key Classes and Functionalities

The Qt Network module encompasses a rich collection of classes and functions that facilitate network interactions. Let's delve into some of the key players:

1. `QNetworkAccessManager`: Acts as the central coordinator for network operations, managing network requests and responses. It handles the complexities of network protocols, authentication, proxy configuration, and connection management, providing a streamlined interface for sending and receiving data over the network.
2. `QNetworkRequest`: Encapsulates the details of a network request, including the URL, headers, and other metadata. It serves as the blueprint for the request, guiding the `QNetworkAccessManager` in its communication with the network.
3. `QNetworkReply`: Represents the response to a network request, encapsulating the received data, headers, and status codes. It provides methods for accessing the response content, monitoring progress, and handling errors.

4. `QTcpSocket` **and** `QUdpSocket`: Enable low-level TCP (Transmission Control Protocol) and UDP (User Datagram Protocol) communication, respectively. These classes provide fine-grained control over network connections, allowing you to implement custom protocols or interact with specific network services.
5. `QNetworkProxy`: Configures proxy settings for network requests, enabling you to route traffic through intermediary servers for various purposes, such as caching, filtering, or anonymization.

Network Protocols: The Language of Communication

The Qt Network module supports a variety of network protocols, enabling your applications to communicate using the most appropriate method for each scenario. Some common protocols include:

- **HTTP and HTTPS**: The foundation of the web, HTTP (Hypertext Transfer Protocol) and its secure counterpart HTTPS (HTTP Secure) enable the exchange of data between web browsers and servers. Qt's

`QNetworkAccessManager` provides convenient functions for sending HTTP requests and handling responses, making it easy to interact with web services and APIs.
- **FTP**: The File Transfer Protocol (FTP) facilitates file transfers between clients and servers. Qt's `QFtp` class simplifies FTP operations, allowing you to upload, download, and manage files on remote servers.
- **TCP and UDP**: These lower-level protocols offer greater flexibility and control over network communication. You can use `QTcpSocket` and `QUdpSocket` to implement custom protocols, interact with specific network services, or build peer-to-peer applications.

Beyond the Basics

The Qt Network module offers additional features and capabilities beyond the core classes and functionalities mentioned above. These include:

- **Network Disk Cache**: Improves performance by caching network responses locally, reducing the need for repeated network requests.

- **Network Authentication**: Supports various authentication mechanisms, such as Basic, Digest, and NTLM, to securely access protected resources.
- **SSL Support**: Enables secure communication over encrypted channels using SSL (Secure Sockets Layer) or TLS (Transport Layer Security).
- **Network Proxies**: Configures and manages network proxies to route traffic through intermediary servers.

Best Practices

To ensure efficient and reliable network communication in your Qt applications, adhere to the following best practices:

- **Asynchronous Operations**: Perform network operations asynchronously to prevent blocking the main thread and ensure a responsive user interface.
- **Error Handling**: Implement robust error handling mechanisms to gracefully manage network errors, such as connection timeouts, server errors, or invalid data.
- **Progress Monitoring**: Provide feedback to the user about the progress of network

operations, especially for lengthy transfers or downloads.
- **Security Considerations**: Employ secure protocols like HTTPS and implement appropriate authentication and authorization mechanisms to protect sensitive data.

The Qt Network module empowers your applications to communicate seamlessly with the world, opening doors to a vast array of online resources and services. By mastering its core components, functionalities, and best practices, you can build networked Qt applications that thrive in the interconnected digital landscape.

In the following sections, we'll explore practical examples of network communication in Qt, demonstrating how to send HTTP requests, handle responses, transfer files via FTP, and implement custom TCP and UDP communication. Get ready to unleash the power of Qt's Network module and connect your applications to the boundless possibilities of the networked world.

Making HTTP Requests

HTTP (Hypertext Transfer Protocol) serves as the foundation of the World Wide Web, enabling the exchange of data between clients (such as web browsers) and servers. In the realm of Qt applications, the `QNetworkAccessManager` class emerges as the key facilitator for making HTTP requests and handling their corresponding responses. This powerful class abstracts the complexities of HTTP communication, providing a streamlined and intuitive interface for interacting with web services, APIs, and other online resources. In this section, we'll delve into the art of making HTTP requests with Qt, exploring the necessary steps, configuration options, and best practices for seamless communication with the web.

The QNetworkAccessManager: Your HTTP Envoy

The `QNetworkAccessManager` class acts as your HTTP envoy, managing the intricacies of network requests and responses. It handles the low-level details of establishing connections, sending requests, receiving responses, and managing cookies, authentication, and other HTTP-related aspects. By leveraging `QNetworkAccessManager`, you can focus on the core logic of your application without getting entangled in the complexities of HTTP communication.

Crafting the QNetworkRequest

Before sending an HTTP request, you need to create a `QNetworkRequest` object that encapsulates the details of the request. This object specifies the URL (Uniform Resource Locator) of the target resource, along with any necessary headers, query parameters, or other metadata.

C++

```
QNetworkAccessManager* manager = new QNetworkAccessManager(this);
QNetworkRequest request(QUrl("https://www.example.com/api/data"));
request.setHeader(QNetworkRequest::ContentTypeHeader, "application/json");
```

In this example, we create a `QNetworkRequest` object for the URL `https://www.example.com/api/data`. We also set the `Content-Type` header to `application/json`, indicating that we're sending JSON-formatted data in the request body.

Sending the Request

Once you have a `QNetworkRequest` object ready, you can send the HTTP request using the `get()`, `post()`, `put()`, or `deleteLater()` methods of the `QNetworkAccessManager`, depending on the desired HTTP method. These methods return a `QNetworkReply` object, which represents the asynchronous response to the request.

C++

```
QNetworkReply* reply = manager->get(request);
connect(reply, &QNetworkReply::finished, this, &MyClass::handleReply);
```

In this example, we send a GET request using the `get()` method and connect the `finished()` signal of the `QNetworkReply` to a slot `handleReply()` that will process the response when it's available.

Handling the Response

The `QNetworkReply` object provides access to the response data, headers, and status codes. You can use its methods to read the response content, check the HTTP status code, and handle any errors that might have occurred during the request.

C++

```
void MyClass::handleReply()
{
          QNetworkReply* reply = qobject_cast<QNetworkReply*>(sender());
          if (reply->error() == QNetworkReply::NoError) {
                QByteArray data = reply->readAll();
      // Process the received data
    } else {
          qDebug() << "Error:" << reply->errorString();
                // Handle the error appropriately
    }
```

```
        reply->deleteLater();
}
```

In this slot function, we retrieve the `QNetworkReply` object from the sender and check if any errors occurred during the request. If the request was successful, we read the response data using `readAll()` and process it accordingly. Otherwise, we handle the error by displaying an error message or taking other appropriate actions. Finally, we delete the `QNetworkReply` object to free up resources.

Asynchronous Operations and Event Loop

HTTP requests in Qt are inherently asynchronous, meaning they don't block the execution of your application while waiting for the response. Instead, the `QNetworkAccessManager` utilizes Qt's event loop to manage network operations in the background, emitting signals when responses are available or errors occur.

This asynchronous behavior ensures that your GUI remains responsive even during lengthy network operations, providing a smooth and user-friendly experience.

Making HTTP requests is a fundamental aspect of interacting with web services and online resources in Qt applications. The `QNetworkAccessManager` class, coupled with `QNetworkRequest` and `QNetworkReply`, provides a powerful and intuitive interface for sending requests, handling responses, and managing the complexities of HTTP communication.

TCP and UDP Communication

While HTTP reigns supreme for web-based interactions, Qt's Network module extends its reach beyond the confines of the World Wide Web, empowering your applications to engage in direct communication with other devices and services through the foundational protocols of TCP (Transmission Control Protocol) and UDP (User Datagram Protocol). These lower-level protocols offer greater flexibility and control over network interactions, enabling you to build custom protocols, interact with specific network services, or establish peer-to-peer communication channels. In this section, we'll delve into the intricacies of TCP and UDP communication in Qt, exploring the key classes, concepts, and techniques for harnessing their power in your applications.

TCP: The Reliable Connection

TCP is a connection-oriented protocol that establishes a reliable, ordered, and error-checked communication channel between two endpoints. It ensures that data is transmitted accurately and completely, making it ideal for applications that require guaranteed delivery and data integrity.

Qt's `QTcpSocket` class encapsulates the functionalities of a TCP socket, providing methods for connecting to a remote host, sending and receiving data, and managing the connection state.

C++

```
QTcpSocket* socket = new QTcpSocket(this);
socket->connectToHost("www.example.com", 80);

connect(socket, &QTcpSocket::connected, this, &MyClass::onConnected);
```

```
connect(socket,
&QTcpSocket::readyRead,           this,
&MyClass::onReadyRead);
connect(socket,
QOverload<QAbstractSocket::SocketError
>::of(&QAbstractSocket::error),
        this, &MyClass::onError);
```

In this example, we create a `QTcpSocket` and initiate a connection to `www.example.com` on port 80. We then connect the socket's `connected`, `readyRead`, and `error` signals to corresponding slots that handle connection establishment, data reception, and error occurrences.

UDP: The Lightweight Datagram

UDP, in contrast to TCP, is a connectionless protocol that transmits data in self-contained packets called datagrams. It prioritizes speed and efficiency over guaranteed delivery, making it suitable for applications where occasional packet loss is tolerable, such as real-time multimedia streaming or gaming.

Qt's `QUdpSocket` class represents a UDP socket, providing methods for binding to a local port, sending and receiving datagrams, and managing multicast communication.

C++

```
QUdpSocket* socket = new QUdpSocket(this);
socket->bind(QHostAddress::AnyIPv4, 45454);

connect(socket, &QUdpSocket::readyRead, this, &MyClass::onReadyRead);
```

In this example, we create a `QUdpSocket` and bind it to any available IPv4 address on port 45454. We then connect the socket's `readyRead` signal to a slot that processes incoming datagrams.

Choosing the Right Protocol

Selecting the appropriate protocol, TCP or UDP, depends on the specific requirements of your application. Consider the following factors:

- **Reliability**: If guaranteed delivery and data integrity are crucial, opt for TCP.
- **Efficiency**: If speed and efficiency are paramount, even at the cost of occasional packet loss, consider UDP.
- **Application Type**: Certain applications, such as file transfers or database interactions, inherently rely on TCP's reliability. Others, like real-time communication or streaming, might benefit from UDP's efficiency.

Beyond the Basics

Qt's Network module offers additional features and capabilities for TCP and UDP communication, including:

- **Multithreading**: Perform network operations in separate threads to prevent blocking the main thread and ensure a responsive user interface.
- **SSL/TLS Support**: Secure TCP connections using SSL (Secure Sockets Layer) or TLS (Transport Layer Security) for encrypted communication.
- **Multicast Communication**: Enable one-to-many or many-to-many communication using UDP multicast.

- **Network Time Protocol (NTP)**: Synchronize your application's clock with a remote NTP server to ensure accurate timekeeping.

Best Practices

To ensure efficient and reliable TCP and UDP communication, adhere to the following best practices:

- **Handle Errors Gracefully**: Implement robust error handling mechanisms to manage connection failures, timeouts, and other network-related issues.
- **Optimize Data Transfer**: Minimize the amount of data transmitted over the network to reduce latency and bandwidth consumption.
- **Consider Security**: Employ secure protocols and authentication mechanisms when transmitting sensitive data.
- **Test Thoroughly**: Rigorously test your TCP and UDP communication under various network conditions to ensure robustness and reliability.

Qt's Network module empowers your applications to transcend the limitations of a single device, enabling seamless communication with other systems and services through the foundational protocols of TCP and UDP. By mastering these protocols and their associated Qt classes, you can build networked applications that exchange data, interact with remote services, and facilitate peer-to-peer communication, opening doors to a world of interconnected possibilities.

Building Networked Applications

With a solid understanding of Qt's Network module and its support for various protocols like HTTP, TCP, and UDP, you're now equipped to embark on the exciting journey of building networked applications. These applications transcend the boundaries of a single device, interacting with remote servers, exchanging data with other clients, and facilitating real-time communication. In this section, we'll explore the art of constructing networked applications in Qt, delving into architectural considerations, design patterns, and practical examples that showcase the power and versatility of Qt's networking capabilities.

Architectural Considerations

The architecture of a networked application plays a crucial role in its functionality, scalability, and maintainability. Qt's Network module provides the building blocks, but it's up to you to assemble them into a cohesive and efficient structure. Consider the following architectural patterns when designing your networked applications:

- **Client-Server Architecture:** The most common pattern, where clients initiate requests to a central server, which processes the requests and sends back responses. This architecture is suitable for applications that require centralized data management, authentication, or resource sharing.
- **Peer-to-Peer Architecture:** In this decentralized model, each node in the network acts as both a client and a server, enabling direct communication and data exchange between peers. This architecture is often used for file sharing, collaborative applications, or distributed systems.
- **Hybrid Architectures:** Combining elements of both client-server and peer-to-peer models, hybrid architectures offer flexibility and adaptability to different scenarios. For instance, an application might use a central server for authentication and data synchronization while allowing direct

peer-to-peer communication for real-time interactions.

Design Patterns: Structuring Your Code

Design patterns provide proven solutions to recurring problems in software development, promoting code reusability, maintainability, and scalability. When building networked applications in Qt, consider employing the following design patterns:

- **Observer Pattern**: Facilitates loose coupling between objects by allowing one object (the subject) to notify other objects (the observers) about changes in its state. This pattern is ideal for handling events and updates in networked applications, such as new messages in a chat application or changes in a shared document.
- **Model-View-Controller (MVC)**: Separates the concerns of data management (model), data presentation (view), and user interaction (controller). This pattern promotes modularity and testability, making it suitable for complex networked applications with multiple views and data sources.

- **Asynchronous Programming**: Qt's event loop and signal-slot mechanism naturally lend themselves to asynchronous programming, where network operations are performed in the background without blocking the main thread. Embrace asynchronous patterns to ensure a responsive and user-friendly experience, even during lengthy network interactions.

Practical Examples

Let's explore a few practical examples of networked applications built with Qt:

- **Chat Application**: A real-time chat application that enables users to exchange messages with each other over a network. This application might utilize TCP or UDP for communication, depending on the desired level of reliability and efficiency.
- **File Sharing Application**: A peer-to-peer file-sharing application that allows users to share files directly with each other. This application might leverage TCP for reliable file transfers and UDP for peer discovery and metadata exchange.

- **Networked Game**: A multiplayer game that connects players over a network, enabling them to interact and compete in real-time. This application might use UDP for low-latency communication and TCP for reliable game state synchronization.

Best Practices

To ensure the success of your networked Qt applications, adhere to the following best practices:

- **Thorough Testing**: Rigorously test your application under various network conditions, including low bandwidth, high latency, and packet loss, to identify and address potential issues.
- **Error Handling and Recovery**: Implement robust error handling mechanisms to gracefully manage network errors and provide informative feedback to the user.
- **Security Considerations**: Employ secure protocols, authentication, and authorization mechanisms to protect sensitive data transmitted over the network.
- **Scalability**: Design your application with scalability in mind, ensuring it can handle

increasing numbers of users and data volumes.
- **User Experience**: Prioritize a seamless and intuitive user experience, even in the face of network challenges or limitations.

Building networked applications with Qt empowers you to create software that transcends the boundaries of a single device, connecting users, sharing data, and facilitating real-time interactions. By embracing Qt's Network module, architectural patterns, design patterns, and best practices, you can craft robust, scalable, and user-friendly networked applications that thrive in the interconnected digital landscape.

Chapter 11: Multithreading: Enhancing Performance

Qt Threading Support

In the realm of modern computing, where multi-core processors reign supreme and user expectations for responsive and performant applications continue to rise, harnessing the power of multithreading becomes paramount. Qt, with its robust threading support, empowers you to create applications that seamlessly execute tasks concurrently, maximizing resource utilization and delivering a smooth and efficient user experience. In this section, we'll delve into the intricacies of Qt's threading support, exploring its core concepts, classes, and best practices for building multithreaded Qt applications that thrive in the multi-core era.

The Essence of Multithreading

Multithreading involves dividing an application's workload into multiple threads of execution that can run concurrently on different processor cores. This parallelism allows you to perform time-consuming or blocking operations in the background without freezing the user interface or hindering the overall responsiveness of your application.

Qt's threading support provides a high-level and platform-independent abstraction for working with threads, encapsulating the complexities of thread creation, synchronization, and communication. It empowers you to focus on the core logic of your application while Qt handles the underlying threading mechanisms transparently.

Key Classes and Concepts

Qt's threading support revolves around a few key classes and concepts:

1. `QThread`: Represents a thread of execution within your Qt application. It provides methods for starting, stopping, and managing the thread's lifecycle, as well as mechanisms for interacting with objects in other threads.
2. `QObject` **and Thread Affinity**: Every `QObject` in Qt has a thread affinity, indicating the thread in which it was created and to which it belongs. Objects with the same thread affinity can communicate directly through signals and slots, while objects in different threads require special mechanisms for safe communication.

3. `moveToThread()`: This crucial function allows you to move a `QObject` from one thread to another, changing its thread affinity and enabling it to execute its slots in the context of the new thread.
4. **Signals and Slots Across Threads**: Qt's signal-slot mechanism extends seamlessly across threads, allowing objects in different threads to communicate safely and efficiently. Qt automatically queues signals emitted from one thread to be delivered to slots in another thread, ensuring thread safety and preventing race conditions.
5. **Synchronization Primitives**: Qt provides various synchronization primitives, such as mutexes, semaphores, and wait conditions, to coordinate access to shared data and prevent data corruption in multithreaded environments.

Threading Models in Qt

Qt offers two primary threading models for structuring your multithreaded applications:

1. **Subclassing** `QThread`: In this model, you create a subclass of `QThread` and override its `run()` method to define the thread's

execution logic. This approach gives you fine-grained control over the thread's behavior but can lead to complexities in managing object ownership and communication across threads.

2. **Worker Objects and** `moveToThread()`: In this model, you create worker objects that encapsulate the tasks to be executed in separate threads. You then move these worker objects to dedicated `QThread` instances using the `moveToThread()` function. This approach promotes cleaner code organization and simplifies communication between threads using signals and slots.

Best Practices

To ensure the success and maintainability of your multithreaded Qt applications, adhere to the following best practices:

- **Minimize Shared Data**: Minimize the amount of data shared between threads to reduce the need for synchronization and avoid potential race conditions.
- **Use Immutable Data When Possible**: If data doesn't need to be modified, consider

making it immutable to eliminate the need for synchronization altogether.
- **Prefer `moveToThread()` over Subclassing `QThread`**: Unless you require very specific control over thread management, opt for the worker object and `moveToThread()` approach for cleaner code and easier communication.
- **Use Signals and Slots for Communication**: Leverage Qt's signal-slot mechanism to communicate safely and efficiently between objects in different threads.
- **Employ Synchronization Primitives When Necessary**: Use mutexes, semaphores, or wait conditions to protect shared data and prevent race conditions when direct communication between threads is unavoidable.
- **Test Thoroughly**: Rigorously test your multithreaded application under various conditions to identify and address potential race conditions, deadlocks, or other threading-related issues.

Qt's threading support empowers you to harness the power of multi-core processors and create responsive and performant applications. By understanding the core concepts, classes, and best practices of Qt threading, you can seamlessly integrate multithreading into your GUI applications, enabling them to execute tasks concurrently, maximize resource utilization, and deliver a smooth and efficient user experience.

QThread and Worker Objects

In the realm of Qt multithreading, the `QThread` class and the concept of worker objects form a dynamic duo, providing a structured and efficient approach to executing tasks concurrently in separate threads. `QThread` represents a thread of execution within your Qt application, while worker objects encapsulate the specific tasks or operations to be performed in that thread. This symbiotic relationship empowers you to delegate time-consuming or blocking operations to background threads, ensuring that your main thread remains responsive and your GUI stays interactive, even during intensive computations or network interactions. In this section, we'll delve into the intricacies of `QThread` and worker objects, exploring their roles, interactions, and best practices for seamlessly integrating them into your Qt applications.

QThread: The Thread Container

The `QThread` class serves as a container for a thread of execution within your Qt application. It provides the necessary infrastructure for creating, starting, stopping, and managing the thread's lifecycle. Each `QThread` instance represents an independent thread that can execute code concurrently with other threads in your application.

While `QThread` itself doesn't execute any code directly, it acts as a vessel for worker objects, which encapsulate the actual tasks to be performed in the thread. By moving worker objects to a `QThread` using the `moveToThread()` function, you effectively delegate their execution to the thread, enabling them to run concurrently with the main thread.

Worker Objects: The Task Executors

Worker objects are `QObject`-derived classes that encapsulate the specific tasks or operations you want to execute in a separate thread. They typically contain slots that perform the actual work, such as complex calculations, file I/O operations, network requests, or any other time-consuming or blocking tasks.

By moving a worker object to a `QThread` using `moveToThread()`, you change its thread affinity, ensuring that its slots are executed in the context of the new thread. This allows you to offload heavy computations or blocking operations to background threads, freeing up the main thread to handle UI updates and user interactions.

The `moveToThread()` Function: The Thread Affinity Changer

The `moveToThread()` function plays a crucial role in establishing the connection between a worker object and a `QThread`. It changes the thread affinity of the worker object, effectively moving it to the specified thread. Once moved, the worker object's slots will be executed in the context of the new thread, enabling concurrent execution and improved responsiveness.

C++

```
MyWorker* worker = new MyWorker;
QThread* thread = new QThread;
worker->moveToThread(thread);
thread->start();
```

In this example, we create a `MyWorker` object and a `QThread`. We then move the `worker` to the `thread` using `moveToThread()`. Finally, we start the `thread`, allowing the `worker`'s slots to be executed concurrently in the new thread.

Communication and Synchronization

Communication between objects in different threads requires careful consideration to ensure thread safety and prevent data races or deadlocks. Qt's signal-slot mechanism extends seamlessly across threads, providing a safe and efficient way for objects to communicate, even when they reside in different threads.

When a signal is emitted from one thread, Qt automatically queues the signal to be delivered to any connected slots in other threads. This ensures that slots are executed in the context of their own threads, preventing concurrent access to shared data and maintaining data integrity.

In scenarios where direct communication between threads is unavoidable, Qt provides synchronization primitives, such as mutexes, semaphores, and wait conditions, to coordinate access to shared data and prevent conflicts.

Best Practices

To ensure effective and maintainable multithreading with `QThread` and worker objects, adhere to the following best practices:

- **Design for Concurrency**: Structure your code and data to minimize dependencies between threads and avoid shared mutable state whenever possible.
- **Use Signals and Slots for Communication**: Leverage Qt's signal-slot mechanism for safe and efficient communication between objects in different threads.
- **Employ Synchronization Primitives When Necessary**: Use mutexes, semaphores, or wait conditions to protect shared data and prevent race conditions when direct communication between threads is unavoidable.
- **Clean Up Threads and Worker Objects**: Ensure proper cleanup of `QThread` objects and worker objects to avoid memory leaks and resource contention.

`QThread` and worker objects provide a structured and efficient approach to multithreading in Qt, enabling you to delegate tasks to background threads and achieve improved performance and responsiveness in your applications. By understanding their roles, interactions, and best practices, you can seamlessly integrate multithreading into your GUI development workflow and create applications that harness the full power of modern multi-core processors.

Synchronizing Threads

In the intricate dance of multithreaded Qt applications, where multiple threads execute concurrently, ensuring harmonious coordination and preventing data corruption becomes paramount. Synchronization mechanisms emerge as the conductors of this symphony, orchestrating access to shared resources and maintaining data integrity in the face of concurrent operations. In this section, we'll explore the art of synchronizing threads in Qt, delving into the essential synchronization primitives, their applications, and best practices for achieving thread-safe and robust multithreaded code.

The Challenge of Shared Data

When multiple threads access and modify the same data simultaneously, conflicts and inconsistencies can arise. This phenomenon, known as a data race, can lead to unpredictable behavior, crashes, and data corruption. To prevent such issues, synchronization mechanisms are employed to control access to shared data, ensuring that only one thread can modify the data at any given time.

Mutexes: The Guardians of Mutual Exclusion

Mutexes (mutual exclusion objects) are fundamental synchronization primitives that provide exclusive access to a shared resource. When a thread acquires a mutex, it gains exclusive ownership of the associated resource, preventing other threads from accessing or modifying it until the mutex is released.

Qt's `QMutex` class encapsulates the functionality of a mutex, offering methods for locking and unlocking the mutex, as well as convenient functions for acquiring the mutex with timeouts or in a non-blocking manner.

C++

```
QMutex mutex;
```

```
void MyWorker::processData() {
    mutex.lock();
    // Access and modify shared data
    mutex.unlock();
}
```

In this example, we use a `QMutex` to protect access to shared data within the `processData()` slot of a worker object. Before accessing or modifying the data, the worker thread acquires the mutex using `lock()`. Once the operations are complete, the mutex is released using `unlock()`, allowing other threads to acquire it and access the shared data.

Semaphores: Counting Access

Semaphores are another synchronization primitive that controls access to a shared resource, but unlike mutexes, they allow a specified number of threads to access the resource concurrently. This is useful in scenarios where you want to limit the number of threads performing a particular operation simultaneously, such as controlling access to a limited pool of resources.

Qt's `QSemaphore` class represents a semaphore, providing methods for acquiring and releasing permits, as well as querying the number of available permits.

C++

```
QSemaphore semaphore(3); // Maximum of 3 threads can access the resource concurrently

void MyWorker::performTask() {
    semaphore.acquire();
    // Access the shared resource
    // ...
    semaphore.release();
}
```

In this example, we create a `QSemaphore` with an initial count of 3, allowing a maximum of three threads to access the shared resource concurrently. Each worker thread acquires a permit using `acquire()` before accessing the resource and releases the permit using `release()` when done, ensuring controlled access and preventing resource contention.

Wait Conditions: Signaling and Waiting

Wait conditions provide a mechanism for threads to wait for specific conditions to become true before proceeding. This is useful in scenarios where one thread needs to wait for another thread to complete a task or modify shared data before it can continue its execution.

Qt's `QWaitCondition` class represents a wait condition, offering methods for signaling and waiting on the condition, as well as specifying timeouts for waiting.

C++

```
QMutex mutex;
QWaitCondition condition;
bool dataReady = false;

void producerThread() {
    // Produce data
    mutex.lock();
    dataReady = true;
    condition.wakeOne(); // Wake up one waiting thread
```

```
    mutex.unlock();
}

void consumerThread() {
    mutex.lock();
    while (!dataReady) {
        condition.wait(&mutex); // Wait for data to be ready
    }
    // Consume data
    mutex.unlock();
}
```

In this example, we have a producer thread that generates data and a consumer thread that processes the data. The `dataReady` flag and the `mutex` ensure that the consumer thread waits until the data is ready before accessing it. The producer thread signals the `condition` using `wakeOne()` to notify the consumer thread that the data is available.

Synchronizing threads is a critical aspect of building robust and reliable multithreaded Qt applications. By understanding the challenges of shared data and mastering the use of synchronization primitives like mutexes, semaphores, and wait conditions, you can ensure thread safety, prevent data corruption, and achieve harmonious coordination between concurrent threads.

Best Practices for Multithreaded Applications

Navigating the intricate landscape of multithreaded Qt applications demands more than just understanding the mechanics of threads and synchronization primitives. It requires adopting a mindset that prioritizes thread safety, efficiency, and maintainability. In this section, we'll distill the wisdom accumulated from countless Qt projects, presenting you with a set of best practices that will empower you to craft multithreaded applications that are not only performant but also robust, scalable, and easy to maintain.

1. **Minimize Shared Data**

The cornerstone of thread safety lies in minimizing the amount of data shared between threads. Shared mutable state introduces the potential for data races and inconsistencies, requiring careful synchronization and meticulous management. Whenever possible, strive to encapsulate data within individual threads, limiting its accessibility and reducing the need for complex synchronization mechanisms.

2. Use Immutable Data When Possible

If data doesn't need to be modified, consider making it immutable, meaning its value cannot be changed after creation. Immutable data eliminates the risk of data races altogether, as multiple threads can safely access it without the need for synchronization.

3. **Prefer** `moveToThread()` **over Subclassing** `QThread`

Unless you require very specific control over thread management, opt for the worker object and `moveToThread()` approach for cleaner code and easier communication. This pattern promotes a clear separation of concerns, encapsulating thread-specific logic within worker objects and delegating their execution to dedicated `QThread` instances.

4. Use Signals and Slots for Communication

Qt's signal-slot mechanism extends seamlessly across threads, providing a safe and efficient way for objects in different threads to communicate. Leverage this powerful mechanism to send notifications, pass data, and trigger actions between threads, ensuring thread safety and preventing race conditions.

5. **Employ Synchronization Primitives When Necessary**

In scenarios where direct communication between threads is unavoidable, use synchronization primitives like mutexes, semaphores, or wait conditions to protect shared data and prevent conflicts. However, exercise caution and strive to minimize the use of these primitives, as excessive synchronization can introduce overhead and hinder performance.

6. **Avoid Blocking the Event Loop**

Qt's event loop is the heart of its responsiveness, handling user input, paint events, and other critical tasks. Avoid performing long-running or blocking operations in the main thread, as this will freeze the GUI and degrade the user experience. Instead, delegate such operations to worker objects running in separate threads, ensuring a smooth and interactive interface.

7. **Clean Up Threads and Worker Objects**

Properly manage the lifecycle of your `QThread` objects and worker objects to prevent memory leaks and resource contention. When a thread is no longer needed, ensure it's terminated gracefully and its associated resources are released. Similarly, delete worker objects when they are no longer required to free up memory and avoid potential dangling references.

8. **Test Thoroughly**

Multithreaded applications are inherently complex and prone to subtle errors that might not manifest in single-threaded scenarios. Rigorously test your application under various conditions, including different thread interleavings and potential race conditions, to identify and address any issues. Qt's testing framework, coupled with debugging tools, can assist you in uncovering and resolving threading-related problems.

9. **Document Threading Interactions**

Clearly document the threading behavior and interactions within your application. This includes specifying which objects belong to which threads, how they communicate, and any synchronization mechanisms employed. Clear documentation facilitates understanding, collaboration, and future maintenance of your codebase.

10. **Stay Informed about Qt's Threading Evolution**

Qt's threading support continues to evolve, with new features and enhancements introduced in each release. Stay abreast of the latest developments by consulting the Qt documentation and exploring online resources. By staying informed, you can leverage the full power of Qt's threading capabilities and create multithreaded applications that are both performant and maintainable.

Building multithreaded Qt applications demands a combination of technical expertise and adherence to best practices. By minimizing shared data, using immutable data, preferring the worker object and `moveToThread()` approach, leveraging signals and slots, employing synchronization primitives judiciously, and testing thoroughly, you can create applications that harness the power of multi-core processors, deliver exceptional performance, and provide a seamless and responsive user experience.

Chapter 12: 3D Graphics with Qt 3D

Introduction to Qt 3D

In the realm of modern user interfaces, where visual richness and immersive experiences are increasingly sought after, the ability to incorporate 3D graphics seamlessly into your Qt applications opens up a world of possibilities. Qt 3D emerges as the enabler of this 3D transformation, providing a powerful and flexible framework for creating, rendering, and interacting with 3D scenes directly within your Qt projects. In this section, we'll embark on an exploration of Qt 3D, unraveling its essence, capabilities, and the transformative impact it can have on your GUI applications.

The Essence of Qt 3D

Qt 3D is a comprehensive 3D framework that empowers you to build and render 3D scenes within your Qt applications, seamlessly blending them with traditional 2D elements to create visually stunning and interactive user experiences. It leverages modern graphics APIs like OpenGL, Vulkan, Metal, and DirectX, providing hardware-accelerated rendering for optimal performance and visual fidelity.

At its core, Qt 3D adopts a scene graph-based approach, where 3D scenes are constructed hierarchically using entities, components, and aspects. Entities represent the objects within the scene, components define their properties and behaviors, and aspects provide additional functionalities like physics, animation, or audio. This modular and extensible architecture allows you to build complex and dynamic 3D scenes with ease, tailoring them to your specific requirements.

Capabilities and Features

Qt 3D boasts a rich set of capabilities and features that empower you to create immersive 3D experiences:

- **2D and 3D Rendering:** Render both 2D and 3D content within the same scene, seamlessly blending traditional Qt Quick elements with 3D objects.
- **Meshes and Geometry:** Define the shape and structure of 3D objects using meshes, which are collections of vertices, edges, and faces. Qt 3D supports various mesh formats, including Wavefront OBJ and glTF, allowing you to import 3D models from external sources.

- **Materials and Textures:** Apply materials and textures to 3D objects to control their visual appearance, adding realism and detail to your scenes. Qt 3D supports a wide range of material types, including Phong, PBR (Physically Based Rendering), and custom shaders.
- **Lighting and Shadows:** Illuminate your scenes with various light sources, such as directional lights, point lights, and spot lights. Qt 3D also supports shadow mapping techniques to create realistic shadows cast by objects in the scene.
- **Cameras and Views:** Control the perspective from which your scene is viewed using cameras. Qt 3D provides various camera types, including perspective cameras and orthographic cameras, allowing you to achieve different visual effects and perspectives.
- **Animations and Transformations:** Animate the properties of 3D objects over time, creating dynamic and engaging scenes. Qt 3D supports keyframe animations, skeletal animations, and morph target animations, enabling you to bring your 3D models to life.
- **Input Handling and Interaction:** Respond to user input, such as mouse clicks or touch

gestures, to interact with 3D objects in your scene. Qt 3D provides mechanisms for picking objects, handling collisions, and implementing custom interaction logic.

Qt 3D and Qt Quick: A Powerful Combination

Qt 3D seamlessly integrates with Qt Quick, allowing you to embed 3D scenes directly within your QML-based user interfaces. This synergy empowers you to create hybrid UIs that blend 2D and 3D elements, opening doors to innovative and visually captivating applications.

Use Cases and Applications

Qt 3D finds applications in a wide range of domains, including:

- **Data Visualization:** Visualize complex data in 3D, such as scientific simulations, medical imaging, or financial charts, to gain deeper insights and understanding.
- **Game Development:** Create interactive 3D games with rich visuals, physics simulations, and immersive gameplay.
- **Virtual and Augmented Reality:** Build virtual and augmented reality experiences that blend the real and digital worlds, offering

new ways to interact with information and environments.
- **Product Design and Visualization:** Showcase 3D models of products or prototypes, enabling interactive exploration and customization.
- **Education and Training:** Develop interactive 3D simulations and visualizations for educational and training purposes, enhancing learning experiences and knowledge retention.

Qt 3D is a powerful and versatile 3D framework that empowers you to create immersive 3D experiences within your Qt applications. By leveraging its scene graph-based architecture, rich feature set, and seamless integration with Qt Quick, you can build visually stunning and interactive UIs that blend 2D and 3D elements, opening doors to a world of possibilities in GUI development.

Creating 3D Scenes

With Qt 3D's foundation established, it's time to breathe life into your applications by crafting captivating 3D scenes. These scenes, built upon a hierarchical structure of entities, components, and aspects, will serve as the canvas for your 3D creations, allowing you to render objects, apply materials, manipulate lighting, and orchestrate interactive experiences that transcend the boundaries of traditional 2D interfaces. In this section, we'll embark on a step-by-step journey into the realm of 3D scene creation, exploring the essential elements and techniques that empower you to construct immersive 3D environments within your Qt applications.

The Scene3D Element: The Foundation

At the core of every Qt 3D scene lies the `Scene3D` QML element. This element acts as the container for all the 3D content within your scene, providing the essential infrastructure for rendering, lighting, and camera management.

QML

```
import QtQuick 2.15
import QtQuick3D 1.15

Scene3D {
    id: scene
    anchors.fill: parent

    // Add entities, components, and aspects here...
```

}

In this example, we create a Scene3D element that fills the entire parent window, setting the stage for our 3D creations.

Entities: The Actors of the Scene

Entities represent the individual objects within your 3D scene, such as cubes, spheres, models, or even lights and cameras. Each entity is defined by its components, which specify its properties, behaviors, and relationships with other entities in the scene.

QML

```
Entity {
    id: myEntity

    components: [
        Mesh {
            // ... mesh data ...
        },
        Material {
```

```
            // ... material properties
...
        },
        Transform {
            // ... position, rotation, and scale ...
        }
    ]
}
```

In this example, we create an `Entity` with an `id` for reference. We then attach three components to the entity: a `Mesh` to define its shape, a `Material` to control its appearance, and a `Transform` to specify its position, rotation, and scale within the scene.

Components: Defining Properties and Behaviors

Components are the building blocks that define the attributes and functionalities of entities within your 3D scene. Qt 3D provides a wide array of built-in components, each serving a specific purpose:

- `Mesh`: Defines the geometry of an entity, specifying its vertices, edges, and faces. You can create meshes programmatically or load them from external files in various formats, such as Wavefront OBJ or glTF.
- `Material`: Controls the visual appearance of an entity, determining how it interacts with light and reflects colors. Qt 3D supports various material types, including Phong, PBR (Physically Based Rendering), and custom shaders.
- `Transform`: Specifies the position, rotation, and scale of an entity within the 3D space. It allows you to manipulate the entity's location, orientation, and size, creating dynamic and interactive scenes.
- `Camera`: Defines the viewpoint from which the scene is rendered. Qt 3D offers different camera types, such as perspective cameras and orthographic cameras, enabling you to achieve various visual perspectives and effects.
- `Light`: Illuminates the scene, casting light and shadows on objects. Qt 3D supports various light types, including directional lights, point lights, and spot lights, allowing you to create realistic and atmospheric lighting.

Aspects: Adding Functionality

Aspects provide additional functionalities to your 3D scenes, such as physics simulations, animation control, or audio playback. They act as independent modules that can be plugged into your scene, enhancing its capabilities and interactivity.

Qt 3D offers several built-in aspects, including:

- `RenderAspect`: Handles the rendering of the 3D scene, utilizing the underlying graphics API for optimal performance and visual quality.
- `InputAspect`: Manages user input, such as mouse clicks, keyboard events, or touch gestures, allowing you to interact with 3D objects in the scene.
- `PhysicsAspect`: Simulates realistic physics behavior, enabling objects to interact with each other and the environment through collisions, gravity, and other forces.
- `AnimationAspect`: Controls the animation of 3D objects, allowing you to create dynamic and engaging scenes with smooth transitions and transformations.
- `AudioAspect`: Provides spatial audio capabilities, enabling you to play sounds and

music within the 3D environment, enhancing immersion and realism.

Creating 3D scenes in Qt 3D involves assembling a hierarchical structure of entities, components, and aspects. The `Scene3D` element acts as the container, entities represent the objects within the scene, components define their properties and behaviors, and aspects provide additional functionalities.

By mastering these fundamental building blocks and leveraging Qt 3D's rich feature set, you can craft immersive 3D environments, seamlessly blending them with traditional 2D elements to create visually stunning and interactive user interfaces.

Animating and Interacting with 3D Objects

In the realm of 3D graphics, static scenes are mere snapshots frozen in time. To truly captivate and engage users, your 3D creations must come alive with motion and interactivity. Qt 3D empowers you to breathe life into your 3D objects, enabling them to move, transform, and respond to user input, creating dynamic and immersive experiences that transcend the boundaries of traditional static displays. In this section, we'll delve into the art of animating and interacting with 3D objects in Qt 3D, exploring the techniques and tools that allow you to orchestrate captivating scenes and foster meaningful user engagement.

Animation: The Illusion of Life

Animation is the art of creating the illusion of movement by rapidly displaying a sequence of slightly different images or frames. In Qt 3D, you can animate various properties of your 3D objects, such as position, rotation, scale, color, or even custom properties, over time, breathing life into your scenes and captivating your audience.

Qt 3D supports several types of animation:

- **Keyframe Animations**: Define a series of keyframes, each specifying a value for a property at a particular point in time. Qt 3D then interpolates between these keyframes to create smooth transitions and transformations.
- **Skeletal Animations**: Animate 3D models with articulated skeletons, enabling realistic movements and deformations based on predefined bone structures and animations.
- **Morph Target Animations**: Blend between different 3D meshes to create smooth

transitions between shapes or expressions, ideal for facial animations or character transformations.

QML Animation System: The Choreographer

Qt Quick's animation system seamlessly integrates with Qt 3D, providing a declarative and intuitive way to define and control animations within your 3D scenes. You can use familiar QML animation elements like `PropertyAnimation`, `NumberAnimation`, and `SequentialAnimation` to orchestrate complex and dynamic behaviors for your 3D objects.

QML

```
import QtQuick 2.15
import QtQuick3D 1.15

Entity {
    // ... other components ...

    Transform {
                        rotation: Qt.quaternionFromEulerAngles(0, rotationAnimation.value, 0)
    }
```

```
PropertyAnimation {
    id: rotationAnimation
    target: myEntity // Assuming
the Entity has an id of 'myEntity'
    property: "rotation"
    from: 0
    to: 360
    duration: 5000
    loops: Animation.Infinite
    }
}
```

In this example, we use a `PropertyAnimation` to animate the `rotation` property of an `Entity`, causing it to rotate continuously around its Y-axis.

Interaction: Engaging the User

Interactivity is key to creating engaging and immersive 3D experiences. Qt 3D's `InputAspect` enables you to capture and respond to user input, such as mouse clicks, keyboard events, or touch gestures, allowing users to manipulate and interact with 3D objects within the scene.

QML

```
import QtQuick 2.15
import QtQuick3D 1.15
import QtQuick.Controls 2.15

Scene3D {
    // ... other components ...

    InputAspect {
        onClicked: {
            // Handle mouse clicks on 3D objects
        }

        onHovered: {
            // Handle mouse hovers over 3D objects
        }
    }
}
```

In this example, we use the `InputAspect` to handle mouse clicks and hovers on 3D objects within the scene. You can implement custom logic within these event handlers to trigger actions, provide feedback, or modify the scene in response to user interactions.

Beyond the Basics

Qt 3D offers additional features and capabilities for animating and interacting with 3D objects, including:

- **Physics-Based Interactions**: Integrate Qt 3D with the Qt Physics module to simulate realistic physics behavior, enabling objects to respond to forces, collisions, and gravity.
- **Custom Shaders**: Create custom shaders using GLSL (OpenGL Shading Language) or other shading languages to achieve unique visual effects and rendering techniques.
- **Scripting and Logic**: Embed JavaScript code within your QML scenes to implement complex animation logic, interaction handling, or procedural generation of 3D content.

Best Practices

To create captivating and performant 3D animations and interactions, adhere to the following best practices:

- **Optimize Performance**: Minimize the number of draw calls, reduce polygon count, and utilize level-of-detail techniques to optimize rendering performance, especially on resource-constrained devices.
- **Prioritize User Experience**: Design intuitive and responsive interactions that provide clear feedback and guide users through the 3D environment.
- **Test on Target Devices**: Thoroughly test your animations and interactions on the target devices to ensure smooth performance and a consistent user experience.
- **Accessibility Considerations**: Make your 3D content accessible to users with disabilities by providing alternative representations or interaction methods.

Animating and interacting with 3D objects breathe life into your Qt 3D scenes, creating dynamic and engaging experiences that captivate and delight users. By mastering the techniques for animation, input handling, and physics-based interactions, you can craft immersive 3D environments that respond to user input, tell stories, and provide unique and memorable experiences.

Integrating 3D Graphics in Your GUI

Qt 3D's true power shines when it seamlessly merges with your Qt Quick-based user interfaces, creating a harmonious blend of 2D and 3D elements that elevate your applications to new levels of visual sophistication and interactivity. This integration empowers you to embed 3D scenes directly within your QML-based UIs, opening doors to innovative designs and captivating user experiences. In this section, we'll explore the techniques and best practices for integrating 3D graphics into your Qt GUI, enabling you to craft hybrid interfaces that seamlessly combine the best of both worlds.

The `Scene3D` Element: The Gateway

The `Scene3D` QML element acts as the gateway for incorporating 3D content into your Qt Quick UIs. It provides a dedicated space within your 2D interface where you can render 3D scenes, complete with entities, components, and aspects. By nesting a `Scene3D` element within your QML layout, you can seamlessly blend 3D graphics with traditional 2D elements like buttons, labels, and text fields.

QML

```
import QtQuick 2.15
import QtQuick3D 1.15
import QtQuick.Controls 2.15

Column {
    Button {
        text: "Rotate Object"
        onClicked: myEntity.rotation.y += 10 // Assuming 'myEntity' is a 3D object
    }

    Scene3D {
        id: scene
        anchors.fill: parent

        // Add 3D entities, components, and aspects here...
        Entity {
            id: myEntity
            // ... 3D object definition ...
        }
    }
}
```

In this example, we embed a `Scene3D` element within a `Column` layout, alongside a button that triggers a rotation of a 3D object within the scene. This demonstrates how you can seamlessly combine 2D and 3D elements, creating interactive interfaces where users can manipulate 3D content using traditional 2D controls.

Synchronizing 2D and 3D

When integrating 3D graphics into your GUI, it's crucial to ensure a smooth and synchronized experience between the 2D and 3D elements. Consider the following:

- **Coordinate Systems**: Understand the relationship between the 2D coordinate system of your Qt Quick UI and the 3D coordinate system of your `Scene3D`. Use appropriate transformations and coordinate mappings to ensure seamless alignment and interaction between 2D and 3D elements.
- **Event Handling**: Implement event handling mechanisms to capture user input, such as mouse clicks or touch gestures, and translate them into meaningful interactions within the 3D scene. Qt's event system and

the `InputAspect` in Qt 3D facilitate this communication.
- **Performance Optimization**: Be mindful of performance considerations when integrating 3D graphics into your GUI. Optimize your 3D scenes, minimize draw calls, and leverage level-of-detail techniques to ensure smooth rendering and a responsive user interface.

Use Cases and Applications

The integration of 3D graphics into Qt Quick UIs opens up a world of possibilities, enabling you to create innovative and visually captivating applications:

- **Data Visualization Dashboards**: Combine interactive 3D charts and graphs with traditional 2D data displays to provide rich and insightful visualizations.
- **Product Configurators**: Embed 3D models of products within your UI, allowing users to explore, customize, and interact with them in real-time.
- **Educational Applications**: Create interactive 3D simulations and visualizations to enhance learning experiences and facilitate understanding of complex concepts.

- **Game Interfaces**: Design intuitive and immersive game interfaces that seamlessly blend 2D controls and menus with 3D game worlds.
- **Virtual and Augmented Reality Applications**: Overlay 3D content onto the real world using Qt's AR (Augmented Reality) module, creating interactive and informative experiences.

Best Practices

To achieve seamless integration of 3D graphics into your Qt GUI, adhere to the following best practices:

- **Plan Your UI Carefully**: Design your interface with both 2D and 3D elements in mind, ensuring a cohesive and balanced visual composition.
- **Optimize for Performance**: Employ efficient rendering techniques, minimize draw calls, and leverage level-of-detail to maintain optimal performance.
- **Prioritize User Experience**: Ensure that interactions between 2D and 3D elements are intuitive, responsive, and provide clear feedback to the user.
- **Test on Target Devices**: Thoroughly test your hybrid UI on the target devices to

identify and address any performance or compatibility issues.

Integrating 3D graphics into your Qt GUI empowers you to create visually stunning and interactive applications that transcend the limitations of traditional 2D interfaces. By embedding `Scene3D` elements within your QML layouts, synchronizing 2D and 3D interactions, and adhering to best practices, you can craft hybrid UIs that seamlessly blend the best of both worlds, delivering captivating and immersive user experiences.

Chapter 13: Qt Quick: Building Fluid UIs

Qt Quick Fundamentals

In the realm of modern user interface design, where fluidity, dynamism, and touch-friendliness reign supreme, Qt Quick emerges as a transformative force, empowering you to craft visually captivating and interactive experiences that resonate with users across a spectrum of devices. Built upon the declarative power of QML and the performance of Qt's underlying C++ engine, Qt Quick provides a streamlined and intuitive framework for building fluid and responsive UIs that adapt seamlessly to different screen sizes, resolutions, and input modalities. In this section, we'll embark on an exploration of Qt Quick fundamentals, unraveling its core concepts, syntax, and the transformative impact it can have on your GUI development endeavors.

The Declarative Paradigm

At the heart of Qt Quick lies its declarative nature, a paradigm that shifts the focus from imperative, step-by-step instructions to a more descriptive and intuitive representation of your UI. In QML, you define *what* you want your UI to look like and *how* it should behave, rather than specifying the precise procedural steps to achieve it. This declarative approach fosters clarity, maintainability, and ease of modification, enabling you to iterate rapidly on your designs and adapt to evolving requirements.

QML: The Language of Expression

Qt Quick leverages the power of QML (Qt Modeling Language), a JavaScript-like declarative language that seamlessly blends visual design and behavioral logic. QML's concise syntax and intuitive structure empower you to describe the visual composition and interactive elements of your UI in a human-readable and easily maintainable format.

Visual Elements: The Building Blocks

Qt Quick provides a rich collection of visual elements, ranging from basic shapes and text to sophisticated controls and animations. These elements, represented by QML types, serve as the building blocks for constructing your UIs. Some essential visual elements include:

- `Rectangle`: A versatile rectangular element used for backgrounds, containers, and other visual components.

- `Text`: Displays text content with customizable font, color, and alignment.
- `Image`: Renders images from various sources, including local files, network resources, or even dynamically generated content.
- `Button`: Provides a clickable element for triggering actions within your application.
- `TextInput`: Enables users to input and edit text.
- `ListView`: Displays scrollable lists of data, ideal for presenting collections of items.
- `GridView`: Arranges items in a grid layout, suitable for image galleries or product catalogs.

Layouts: Organizing Your UI

Qt Quick inherits Qt's powerful layout system, allowing you to arrange visual elements in a structured and responsive manner. Layouts automatically adjust the size and position of elements based on the available space, ensuring a visually pleasing and adaptable interface across different screen configurations.

Some common layout types in Qt Quick include:

- `ColumnLayout`: Arranges elements vertically in a single column.
- `RowLayout`: Arranges elements horizontally in a single row.
- `GridLayout`: Organizes elements in a grid-like structure with rows and columns.

Property Bindings: Dynamic Behavior

Qt Quick's property binding system lies at the heart of its dynamic capabilities. Property bindings establish relationships between properties, enabling elements to react and update automatically in response to changes in data, user interactions, or other events.

QML

```
import QtQuick 2.15

Rectangle {
    width: 200
    height: 100
    color: mouseArea.pressed ? "red" : "blue"

    MouseArea {
        anchors.fill: parent
    }
```

}

In this example, the `color` property of the `Rectangle` is bound to a JavaScript expression that evaluates whether the `MouseArea` is pressed. This creates a dynamic behavior where the rectangle changes color when the user interacts with it.

States, Transitions, and Animations: Adding Flair

Qt Quick's state, transition, and animation framework empowers you to create visually captivating and interactive UIs. States represent different visual configurations of your UI, transitions define how the UI smoothly moves between states, and animations add dynamic effects and transformations to elements within your scenes.

QML

```
import QtQuick 2.15

Rectangle {
    width: 100
```

```
    height: 100
    color: "blue"

    states: [
        State {
            name: "expanded"
            PropertyChanges { target: myRectangle; width: 200 }
        }
    ]

    transitions: [
        Transition {
            from: "*"
            to: "expanded"
            NumberAnimation { properties: "width"; duration: 500 }
        }
    ]

    MouseArea {
        anchors.fill: parent
        onClicked: myRectangle.state = "expanded"
    }
}
```

In this example, we define two states for a `Rectangle`: the default state and an "expanded" state where its width is doubled. A transition with a `NumberAnimation` smoothly animates the width change when the user clicks on the rectangle.

Qt Quick, with its declarative paradigm, QML language, visual elements, layouts, property bindings, and animation framework, provides a powerful and intuitive toolkit for building fluid and responsive user interfaces. By mastering these fundamental concepts, you can craft modern, touch-friendly UIs that adapt seamlessly to different screen sizes and resolutions, delivering captivating and engaging user experiences.

Qt Quick Controls

In the pursuit of crafting visually appealing and user-friendly interfaces, Qt Quick Controls emerge as a valuable asset, offering a collection of pre-built UI elements that seamlessly blend with Qt Quick's declarative power and flexibility. These controls encompass a wide range of essential components, from buttons and sliders to menus and dialogs, providing a solid foundation for building intuitive and interactive user experiences. In this section, we'll delve into the world of Qt Quick Controls, exploring their purpose, types, customization options, and practical applications in enriching your QML-based UIs.

The Purpose of Qt Quick Controls

Qt Quick Controls bridge the gap between the low-level visual elements of Qt Quick and the higher-level UI components commonly found in traditional desktop applications. They encapsulate familiar UI elements like buttons, text fields, sliders, and menus, providing a convenient and consistent way to incorporate these essential components into your QML-based interfaces.

By leveraging Qt Quick Controls, you can:

- **Accelerate development:** Utilize pre-built UI elements, eliminating the need to create custom components from scratch.
- **Ensure consistency:** Maintain a cohesive and familiar look and feel across your application, adhering to platform-specific design guidelines.
- **Enhance usability:** Benefit from the built-in accessibility and usability features of Qt

Quick Controls, ensuring your UIs are inclusive and user-friendly.
- **Simplify styling:** Customize the appearance of controls using Qt's stylesheet system or by creating custom styles, tailoring them to your application's aesthetic vision.

Types of Qt Quick Controls

Qt Quick Controls offer a diverse range of UI elements, catering to various interaction patterns and use cases. Some essential control types include:

- **Buttons**: `Button`, `ToolButton`, `RadioButton`, `CheckBox` - Trigger actions, toggle options, and select choices.
- **Input Fields**: `TextField`, `TextArea`, `SpinBox`, `ComboBox`, `Slider` - Capture and display textual or numerical input, select options from lists, or adjust values within a range.
- **Display Elements**: `Label`, `ProgressBar`, `BusyIndicator` - Present information, indicate progress, or visualize activity.
- **Containers**: `Pane`, `ScrollView`, `SplitView`, `TabView` - Organize and arrange other UI elements, provide scrolling

capabilities, or divide the screen into sections.
- **Menus and Dialogs**: `Menu`, `MenuBar`, `ContextMenu`, `Dialog`, `FileDialog`, `ColorDialog` - Present options, display contextual menus, or facilitate user input and feedback through dialog boxes.

Customization and Styling

Qt Quick Controls are highly customizable, allowing you to tailor their appearance and behavior to match your application's design requirements. You can achieve customization through:

- **Properties:** Modify properties like `text`, `color`, `font`, `icon`, and `layout` to adjust the visual presentation and arrangement of controls.
- **Stylesheets:** Apply CSS-like stylesheets to define global or targeted styles for your controls, achieving consistency and visual coherence across your UI.
- **Custom Styles:** Create your own custom styles by subclassing `QQuickStyle` or leveraging Qt's style plugins, enabling you to craft unique and branded looks for your applications.

- **Templates and Delegates:** Customize the internal structure and rendering of controls by defining templates or delegates, providing fine-grained control over their appearance and behavior.

Practical Applications

Qt Quick Controls find applications in a wide range of scenarios, including:

- **Desktop Applications**: Build traditional desktop applications with familiar UI elements like menus, toolbars, and dialogs.
- **Mobile and Embedded Applications**: Craft touch-friendly interfaces for mobile devices and embedded systems, leveraging Qt Quick Controls' adaptability and responsiveness.
- **Hybrid Applications**: Combine Qt Quick Controls with custom QML elements or even 3D graphics using Qt 3D to create unique and visually rich user experiences.
- **Prototyping and Rapid Development**: Utilize Qt Quick Controls to quickly assemble functional prototypes and iterate on your UI designs.

Best Practices

To maximize the benefits of Qt Quick Controls, consider the following best practices:

- **Choose the Right Controls**: Select controls that align with the platform's design guidelines and your application's interaction patterns.
- **Maintain Consistency**: Strive for a consistent look and feel across your UI by using stylesheets or custom styles.
- **Prioritize Usability**: Ensure your controls are accessible, intuitive, and provide clear feedback to the user.
- **Optimize Performance**: Be mindful of performance considerations, especially when using complex controls or animations.

Qt Quick Controls offer a bridge between the declarative power of QML and the familiarity of traditional UI elements, empowering you to build intuitive, interactive, and visually appealing interfaces with ease. By leveraging their pre-built components, customization options, and seamless integration with Qt Quick, you can accelerate development, ensure consistency, and craft user experiences that delight and engage.

Animations and Transitions

In the realm of modern user interfaces, where dynamism and visual appeal reign supreme, animations and transitions emerge as powerful tools for captivating users and enhancing their experience. Qt Quick, with its built-in animation and transition framework, empowers you to breathe life into your UIs, creating smooth and engaging effects that delight and guide users through your application. In this section, we'll delve into the art of animations and transitions in Qt Quick, exploring their types, properties, and practical applications in crafting fluid and visually captivating user interfaces.

The Magic of Animations

Animations in Qt Quick involve the gradual change of one or more properties of a QML element over a specified duration. These properties can encompass position, size, opacity, color, rotation, or any other animatable attribute. By smoothly transitioning between property values, animations create the illusion of movement, transformation, or other visual effects, adding a touch of magic to your UIs.

Qt Quick offers a variety of animation types, each catering to different visual effects and use cases:

- **PropertyAnimation**: The most versatile animation type, `PropertyAnimation` allows you to animate any property of a QML element. You can specify the starting and ending values of the property, the duration of the animation, and various easing curves to control the timing and smoothness of the transition.
- **NumberAnimation**: A specialized animation type for animating numeric properties, such as position, size, or opacity. It provides convenient shortcuts for defining common animation patterns, such as easing in, easing out, or bouncing.
- **ColorAnimation**: Designed for animating color properties, `ColorAnimation` smoothly transitions between different colors, creating visually pleasing fades or color changes.
- **RotationAnimation**: Animates the rotation of an element around a specified axis, enabling spinning, tilting, or other rotational effects.
- **SequentialAnimation** and **ParallelAnimation**: Combine multiple

animations to create complex sequences or simultaneous effects. `SequentialAnimation` executes its child animations one after the other, while `ParallelAnimation` runs its child animations concurrently.

Transitions: Guiding the Flow

Transitions in Qt Quick define how your UI smoothly moves between different states, providing visual continuity and guiding the user's attention. They are triggered by state changes and can involve animations, property changes, or even the creation and destruction of elements.

Qt Quick offers several transition types:

- **Transition**: The base transition type, allowing you to define animations or property changes that occur when a state change is triggered.
- **SequentialTransition** and **ParallelTransition**: Combine multiple transitions to create complex sequences or simultaneous effects, similar to their animation counterparts.
- **AnchorAnimation**: Animates the anchor properties of an element, controlling its

position and alignment relative to other elements.

States: Defining Visual Configurations

States in Qt Quick represent different visual configurations of your UI. By defining states and associating them with specific conditions or user interactions, you can create dynamic interfaces that adapt to different contexts or user preferences.

QML

```
import QtQuick 2.15

Rectangle {
    width: 100
    height: 100
    color: "blue"

    states: [
        State {
            name: "expanded"
            PropertyChanges { target: myRectangle; width: 200 }
        }
    ]

    transitions: [
```

```
        Transition {
            from: "*"
            to: "expanded"
                    NumberAnimation {
properties: "width"; duration: 500 }
            }
    ]

    MouseArea {
        anchors.fill: parent
        onClicked: myRectangle.state = "expanded"
    }
}
```

In this example, we define two states for a `Rectangle`: the default state and an "expanded" state where its width is doubled. A transition with a `NumberAnimation` smoothly animates the width change when the user clicks on the rectangle, creating a visually pleasing and interactive effect.

Best Practices

To create effective and performant animations and transitions, adhere to the following best practices:

- **Purposeful Animations**: Use animations to enhance user experience, provide feedback, or guide attention, rather than just for visual flair.
- **Smooth Transitions**: Employ easing curves and appropriate durations to create smooth and natural transitions between states.
- **Performance Optimization**: Be mindful of performance, especially when using complex animations or transitions on resource-constrained devices.
- **Accessibility Considerations**: Ensure that animations and transitions don't create accessibility barriers for users with disabilities. Provide alternative ways to access content or functionality if needed.

Animations and transitions are the magic wands that transform static Qt Quick UIs into dynamic and engaging experiences. By mastering the art of animation, utilizing states and transitions effectively, and adhering to best practices, you can create interfaces that captivate users, guide their attention, and provide a delightful and memorable experience.

Building Touch-friendly Interfaces

In the era of smartphones and tablets, where touchscreens have become the primary mode of interaction, crafting user interfaces that respond seamlessly to touch gestures is essential. Qt Quick, with its inherent touch support and intuitive gesture handling mechanisms, empowers you to build touch-friendly interfaces that feel natural and intuitive on mobile devices and touch-enabled displays. In this section, we'll explore the techniques and best practices for creating touch-centric UIs in Qt Quick, ensuring your applications deliver a delightful and engaging experience on touchscreens.

Embrace Touch Events

Qt Quick's event system seamlessly handles touch events, providing a foundation for building touch-friendly interfaces. Key touch events include:

- `TouchPoint`: Represents a single point of contact on the touchscreen.
- `TouchEvent`: Encapsulates a collection of touch points, representing a single touch interaction.

- `PinchEvent`: Represents a pinch gesture, typically used for zooming or scaling content.
- `FlickEvent`: Represents a flick gesture, often used for scrolling or navigating through lists.

By handling these touch events and interpreting their associated gestures, you can create interfaces that respond intuitively to the user's touch input.

Gesture Recognition and Handling

Qt Quick's `PinchArea` and `Flickable` elements simplify the implementation of common touch gestures like pinch-to-zoom and flick-to-scroll. These elements automatically recognize and handle the corresponding gestures, providing a smooth and natural user experience.

QML

```
import QtQuick 2.15

PinchArea {
    anchors.fill: parent

    Image {
        source: "image.jpg"
        anchors.centerIn: parent
```

```
        transform: Scale {
            origin.x: image.width / 2
            origin.y: image.height / 2
            xScale: pinch.scale
            yScale: pinch.scale
        }
    }
}
```

In this example, the `PinchArea` element enables pinch-to-zoom functionality for an `Image`. The `pinch.scale` property, automatically updated by the `PinchArea`, controls the scaling of the image, providing a responsive and intuitive zooming experience.

Designing for Touch

When building touch-friendly interfaces, consider the following design principles:

- **Ample Touch Targets**: Ensure that interactive elements, such as buttons or list items, are large enough to be easily tapped

with a finger. Aim for a minimum touch target size of 44x44 pixels.
- **Clear Visual Feedback**: Provide visual cues, such as highlighting or animations, to indicate that an element is interactive and has been touched.
- **Intuitive Gestures**: Utilize gestures that are familiar and natural to users, such as tapping, swiping, pinching, and dragging.
- **Consistent Navigation**: Implement consistent navigation patterns, such as back buttons or swipe gestures, to facilitate easy movement through your application.
- **Minimize Text Input**: Reduce the need for on-screen keyboards by providing alternative input methods, such as voice recognition or selection from lists.

Testing and Iteration

Thoroughly test your touch-friendly interfaces on actual touch-enabled devices to ensure a smooth and intuitive user experience. Pay attention to touch target sizes, gesture recognition accuracy, and overall responsiveness. Iterate on your design based on user feedback and testing results, refining the touch interactions until they feel natural and effortless.

Beyond the Basics

Qt Quick offers additional features and capabilities for building touch-friendly interfaces, including:

- **Multi-touch Support**: Handle multiple simultaneous touch points, enabling gestures like two-finger rotation or multi-finger swiping.
- **Custom Gestures**: Implement custom gesture recognition using Qt's `Gesture` QML type or by subclassing `QGestureRecognizer` in C++, allowing you to create unique and specialized touch interactions.
- **Haptic Feedback**: Provide tactile feedback to users through vibrations or other haptic effects, enhancing the sense of touch and improving the overall user experience.

Building touch-friendly interfaces is essential for creating engaging and intuitive experiences on modern touch-enabled devices. Qt Quick, with its inherent touch support, gesture handling mechanisms, and design flexibility, empowers you to craft UIs that respond seamlessly to touch input and delight users with their natural and fluid interactions.

By embracing touch events, leveraging gesture recognition elements, adhering to touch-centric design principles, and testing thoroughly on actual devices, you can build Qt Quick applications that feel native and intuitive on touchscreens, setting a new standard for user experience in the mobile and touch-enabled world.

Part IV: Real-world Projects

Chapter 14: Building a Cross-platform Media Player

Project Overview and Requirements

In the world of multimedia, the ability to enjoy your favorite audio and video content seamlessly across different devices and operating systems is a coveted feature. In this chapter, we embark on an exciting project to build a cross-platform media player using the power of Qt and C++. By leveraging Qt's multimedia capabilities and cross-platform compatibility, we'll create a versatile media player that delivers a consistent and enjoyable user experience across Windows, macOS, and Linux.

Project Goals

Our primary goal is to develop a media player that supports the playback of various audio and video formats, provides essential playback controls, and offers a user-friendly interface that is both aesthetically pleasing and intuitive to navigate. Additionally, we'll focus on cross-platform compatibility, ensuring that our media player functions seamlessly on different operating systems without requiring any code modifications.

Functional Requirements

Let's outline the core functionalities that our media player should encompass:

- **Media Playback**:
    - Support for popular audio formats (e.g., MP3, WAV, FLAC) and video formats (e.g., MP4, AVI, MKV).
    - Ability to open media files from local storage or network streams.
    - Basic playback controls: play, pause, stop, seek, volume adjustment.
    - Playlist management: create, load, and save playlists.
    - Support for subtitles and closed captions.
- **User Interface**:
    - Intuitive and visually appealing interface.
    - Display of media metadata (e.g., title, artist, album, duration).
    - Visualization of audio waveforms or video thumbnails.
    - Full-screen playback support.
    - Customizable themes or skins.
- **Cross-platform Compatibility**:
    - Seamless functionality on Windows, macOS, and Linux.

- Consistent look and feel across different platforms.
- Adaptation to platform-specific UI guidelines.

Non-functional Requirements

In addition to functional requirements, let's consider some important non-functional aspects:

- **Performance**: The media player should deliver smooth and responsive playback, even for high-resolution video content.
- **Usability**: The interface should be intuitive and easy to navigate, catering to users of varying technical expertise.
- **Accessibility**: The media player should be accessible to individuals with disabilities, providing support for screen readers and other assistive technologies.
- **Maintainability**: The codebase should be well-structured, modular, and documented, facilitating future enhancements and bug fixes.

Technology Stack

We'll leverage the following technologies to build our cross-platform media player:

- **Qt 6**: The core framework for GUI development, multimedia handling, and cross-platform compatibility.
- **C++**: The programming language for implementing the application logic and interacting with Qt's APIs.
- **Qt Multimedia Module**: Provides classes for media playback, playlist management, and audio/video effects.
- **Qt Widgets or Qt Quick**: Choose the appropriate UI toolkit based on your design preferences and target platforms. Qt Widgets offers a traditional desktop-oriented approach, while Qt Quick enables the creation of fluid and touch-friendly interfaces.
- **Third-Party Libraries (Optional)**: Consider using external libraries for advanced features like video decoding, audio processing, or subtitle rendering, depending on your project's specific needs.

Project Structure

We'll adopt a modular and organized project structure to facilitate code maintainability and scalability. The project will likely comprise the following components:

- **Main Window**: The central window of the application, housing the UI elements and coordinating the overall functionality.
- **Media Player Engine**: The core component responsible for media playback, handling file loading, decoding, and rendering.
- **Playlist Manager**: Manages the playlist, allowing users to create, load, and save playlists.
- **UI Components**: Widgets or QML elements for constructing the user interface, including playback controls, media information display, and playlist visualization.

Development Approach

We'll adopt an iterative and incremental development approach, starting with basic playback functionalities and gradually adding more advanced features as we progress. We'll leverage Qt Creator's powerful IDE to design the UI, write C++ code, and debug the application throughout the development process.

Building a cross-platform media player is an ambitious yet rewarding project that showcases the power and versatility of Qt. By adhering to the functional and non-functional requirements, leveraging Qt's multimedia capabilities, and adopting a structured development approach, we'll create a media player that delivers a seamless and enjoyable user experience across different platforms.

Designing the User Interface

A media player's user interface serves as the gateway through which users interact with and control their audio and video content. It should be intuitive, visually appealing, and responsive, providing easy access to playback controls, media information, and playlist management features. In this section, we'll embark on the creative process of designing the user interface for our cross-platform media player, exploring layout considerations, widget selection, and aesthetic choices that contribute to a seamless and enjoyable user experience.

Layout and Structure

The layout of our media player's interface should prioritize clarity and organization, presenting information in a logical and visually pleasing manner. We'll employ Qt's layout managers to arrange widgets strategically, ensuring adaptability to different screen sizes and resolutions.

A typical media player interface might include the following sections:

- **Media Playback Area**: The central focal point, displaying the video content or visualization for audio playback.
- **Playback Controls**: Essential controls for play, pause, stop, seek, volume adjustment, and potentially others like full-screen toggle or playlist navigation.
- **Media Information Display**: Shows relevant metadata about the currently playing media, such as title, artist, album, duration, and progress.
- **Playlist View**: Presents the playlist, allowing users to browse, add, remove, and reorder media files.
- **Additional Features**: Depending on the project scope, you might include sections for equalizer settings, audio/video effects, or other advanced functionalities.

Widget Selection

Qt offers a rich collection of widgets that can be utilized to construct the various sections of our media player's interface. Here are some common choices:

- **Media Playback Area**:
    - `QVideoWidget` (for video playback)
    - `QWidget` with custom painting (for audio visualization)
- **Playback Controls**:
    - `QPushButton` (for play, pause, stop, etc.)
    - `QSlider` (for volume control and seek bar)
- **Media Information Display**:
    - `QLabel` (for displaying text information)
    - `QProgressBar` (for visualizing playback progress)
- **Playlist View**:
    - `QListWidget` or `QTableView` (for displaying the playlist)
- **Additional Features**:
    - `QDial` or `QSlider` (for equalizer adjustments)
    - `QComboBox` or `QListWidget` (for selecting audio/video effects)

Aesthetic Choices

The visual style of your media player can significantly impact the user experience. Consider the following aesthetic choices:

- **Color Scheme**: Choose a color palette that complements the media content and creates a visually pleasing atmosphere.
- **Font Selection**: Select fonts that are legible and enhance the overall aesthetic.
- **Iconography**: Utilize icons to represent actions and functionalities, enhancing visual communication and reducing clutter.
- **Layout Spacing and Margins**: Pay attention to spacing and margins between widgets to ensure a balanced and visually pleasing composition.
- **Visual Effects**: Employ subtle animations or transitions to enhance user feedback and create a sense of dynamism.

Cross-platform Considerations

When designing the UI, it's crucial to consider cross-platform compatibility. Strive for a consistent look and feel across different operating systems while adapting to platform-specific UI guidelines. Qt's style system and layout managers can assist in achieving this balance.

User-Centric Design

Ultimately, the success of your media player's UI hinges on its usability and user-friendliness.

Conduct user research, gather feedback, and iterate on your design to ensure it meets the needs and expectations of your target audience.

Designing the user interface for our cross-platform media player is a creative endeavor that blends functionality, aesthetics, and user-centric principles. By carefully considering layout, widget selection, and visual style, we can create an interface that is both intuitive and visually appealing, providing a seamless and enjoyable experience for users across different platforms.

Implementing Media Playback

At the core of any media player lies the engine that drives the playback of audio and video content. In this section, we'll delve into the implementation details of our media player's playback functionality, leveraging Qt's Multimedia module to handle file loading, decoding, rendering, and control. We'll explore the key classes, techniques, and considerations involved in building a robust and versatile media playback engine that delivers a seamless and enjoyable user experience.

The QMediaPlayer Class: The Playback Maestro

Qt's `QMediaPlayer` class emerges as the central orchestrator of media playback, providing a high-level interface for controlling audio and video playback, managing playlists, and handling media-related events. It abstracts the complexities of media decoding and rendering, allowing you to focus on the core logic of your application without getting entangled in low-level multimedia intricacies.

Loading Media

To initiate playback, you first need to load a media file or network stream into the `QMediaPlayer`. Qt supports various media sources, including local files, URLs, and even custom data streams.

C++

```cpp
QMediaPlayer* player = new QMediaPlayer(this);
player->setMedia(QUrl::fromLocalFile("my_video.mp4"));
```

In this example, we create a `QMediaPlayer` object and load a local video file using the `setMedia()`

function. Qt's multimedia framework automatically handles the decoding and preparation of the media for playback.

Playback Controls

The `QMediaPlayer` class offers a comprehensive set of methods for controlling playback:

- `play()`: Starts or resumes playback.
- `pause()`: Pauses playback.
- `stop()`: Stops playback and resets the position to the beginning.
- `setPosition()`: Seeks to a specific position within the media.
- `setVolume()`: Adjusts the playback volume.
- `setMuted()`: Mutes or unmutes the audio output.

You can connect these methods to buttons or other UI elements in your interface to provide intuitive playback control to the user.

Media State and Events

The `QMediaPlayer` emits various signals to notify your application about changes in its state or the occurrence of media-related events. Some key signals include:

- `stateChanged()`: Emitted when the player's state changes (e.g., from Stopped to Playing).
- `positionChanged()`: Emitted periodically during playback to indicate the current playback position.
- `durationChanged()`: Emitted when the duration of the media is determined.
- `errorOccurred()`: Emitted when an error occurs during playback.

By connecting to these signals, you can update your UI, display progress information, or handle errors gracefully.

Playlist Management

Qt's `QMediaPlaylist` class facilitates the management of playlists, allowing users to create, load, and save collections of media files. You can add media sources to the playlist, control playback order, and handle playlist-related events.

C++

```
QMediaPlaylist* playlist = new
QMediaPlaylist(this);
playlist->addMedia(QUrl::fromLocalFile
("song1.mp3"));
playlist->addMedia(QUrl::fromLocalFile
("song2.mp3"));

player->setPlaylist(playlist);
```

In this example, we create a `QMediaPlaylist`, add two audio files to it, and set it as the playlist for our `QMediaPlayer`. The player will then automatically play the media files in the playlist sequentially.

Cross-platform Considerations

When implementing media playback, it's crucial to consider cross-platform compatibility. Different operating systems might have varying support for media formats and codecs. Qt's multimedia framework abstracts these differences to a certain extent, but you might still need to handle platform-specific quirks or provide alternative playback solutions for unsupported formats.

Performance Optimization

Media playback, especially for high-resolution video content, can be computationally intensive. Optimize your implementation by:

- **Hardware Acceleration**: Leverage hardware-accelerated decoding and rendering whenever possible.
- **Efficient Buffering**: Implement appropriate buffering strategies to minimize playback interruptions and ensure smooth streaming.
- **Multithreading**: Consider offloading media decoding or processing to separate threads to avoid blocking the main thread and maintain GUI responsiveness.

Implementing media playback is a core aspect of building a versatile and user-friendly media player. Qt's `QMediaPlayer` class, coupled with `QMediaPlaylist` and other multimedia components, provides a powerful toolkit for handling media loading, playback control, playlist management, and event handling.

Cross-platform Considerations

Embarking on the journey of cross-platform development with Qt offers the allure of reaching a broader audience with a single codebase. However, this endeavor is not without its challenges. Different operating systems exhibit subtle variations in their file systems, UI guidelines, and multimedia capabilities. In this section, we'll navigate the intricacies of cross-platform development, equipping you with the knowledge and strategies to ensure your media player functions seamlessly and delivers a consistent user experience across Windows, macOS, and Linux.

File Paths and Conventions

File paths and directory structures can vary across operating systems. To ensure your media player can locate and access media files correctly, consider the following:

- **Use Qt's Cross-Platform APIs:** Leverage Qt's `QDir` and `QFile` classes, which provide platform-independent abstractions for file system operations.
- **Handle Path Separators:** Use `QDir::separator()` to obtain the correct path separator for the current platform, ensuring proper file path construction.
- **Consider Case Sensitivity:** File systems on macOS and Linux are case-sensitive, while

Windows is case-insensitive. Be mindful of this when handling file names and paths.

UI Guidelines and Styling

Each operating system has its own set of UI guidelines and visual styles. To create a native look and feel for your media player on each platform, consider the following:

- **Qt Style Sheets**: Utilize Qt style sheets to customize the appearance of your widgets and adapt them to the visual style of the target platform.
- **Platform-Specific Styling:** Explore Qt's built-in styles, such as `Fusion`, `Windows`, or `macOS`, to achieve a native look and feel on each platform.
- **Layout Adjustments**: Fine-tune your layouts and widget sizes to accommodate differences in font rendering, DPI settings, and window decorations across platforms.

Multimedia Capabilities

While Qt's Multimedia module provides a cross-platform foundation for media handling, there might be subtle variations in codec support and hardware acceleration across different operating systems. Consider the following:

- **Codec Availability**: Ensure that the media formats and codecs you intend to support are widely available on all target platforms.
- **Hardware Acceleration**: Leverage hardware-accelerated decoding and rendering whenever possible, but provide fallback mechanisms for platforms with limited hardware support.
- **Platform-Specific Optimizations**: Explore platform-specific optimizations or configurations to enhance media playback performance on each operating system.

Testing and Deployment

Thorough testing on all target platforms is crucial for ensuring cross-platform compatibility. Deploy your media player on Windows, macOS, and Linux machines, and meticulously test its functionality, performance, and visual appearance. Address any platform-specific issues that arise, ensuring a consistent and enjoyable user experience across all environments.

Embrace Qt's Cross-Platform Philosophy

Qt's design philosophy revolves around cross-platform compatibility. By adhering to Qt's best practices and leveraging its platform-independent APIs, you can minimize the need for conditional code and platform-specific workarounds. This streamlines your development process and empowers you to create applications that truly shine on any operating system.

Building a cross-platform media player demands careful attention to the nuances of different operating systems. By addressing file system variations, adapting to UI guidelines, considering multimedia capabilities, and conducting thorough testing, you can ensure that your media player delivers a seamless and consistent user experience across Windows, macOS, and Linux.

Qt's cross-platform framework provides a solid foundation for achieving this goal, empowering you to focus on the core functionalities of your application while minimizing platform-specific complexities. Embrace Qt's cross-platform philosophy, and let it guide you in building media players that transcend boundaries and delight users on any device.

Chapter 15: Developing a Custom Image Editor

Project Overview and Requirements

In the realm of digital creativity, image editing software plays a pivotal role, empowering users to transform and enhance their visual creations. In this chapter, we embark on an exciting project to build a custom image editor using the power and flexibility of Qt and C++. By leveraging Qt's graphics capabilities and intuitive UI framework, we'll craft an image editor that provides essential editing tools, supports various image formats, and offers a user-friendly interface that caters to both novice and experienced users.

Project Goals

Our primary goal is to develop an image editor that empowers users to perform common image editing tasks, such as cropping, resizing, rotating, adjusting colors, applying filters, and adding text or annotations. Additionally, we'll focus on providing a user-friendly interface that is both intuitive and visually appealing, enabling users to unleash their creativity and achieve their desired image transformations effortlessly.

Functional Requirements

Let's outline the core functionalities that our custom image editor should encompass:

- **Image Loading and Saving**:
    - Support for popular image formats (e.g., JPEG, PNG, BMP, GIF).
    - Ability to open images from local storage or network sources.
    - Save edited images in the original or a different format.
- **Basic Editing Tools**:
    - Crop: Select and crop a specific region of the image.
    - Resize: Adjust the dimensions of the image.
    - Rotate: Rotate the image by a specified angle.
    - Flip: Flip the image horizontally or vertically.
- **Color Adjustments**:
    - Brightness: Adjust the overall brightness of the image.
    - Contrast: Modify the contrast between light and dark areas.
    - Saturation: Control the intensity of colors.
    - Hue: Shift the overall color tone.

- **Filters and Effects**:
    - Apply various filters and effects, such as grayscale, sepia, blur, sharpen, or emboss.
    - Provide customizable parameters for fine-tuning the filter effects.
- **Text and Annotations**:
    - Add text overlays to the image with customizable fonts, colors, and styles.
    - Draw shapes, lines, or arrows on the image to annotate or highlight specific areas.
- **User Interface**:
    - Intuitive and visually appealing interface.
    - Clear organization of editing tools and features.
    - Support for undo and redo operations.
    - Zoom and pan functionality for precise editing.
    - Customizable toolbars or menus.

Non-functional Requirements

In addition to functional requirements, let's consider some essential non-functional aspects:

- **Performance**: The image editor should handle image processing operations

efficiently, providing a responsive and smooth user experience.
- **Usability**: The interface should be intuitive and easy to navigate, catering to users of varying technical expertise.
- **Extensibility**: The codebase should be modular and well-structured, allowing for easy addition of new features or plugins in the future.

Technology Stack

We'll leverage the following technologies to build our custom image editor:

- **Qt 6**: The core framework for GUI development, graphics handling, and cross-platform compatibility.
- **C++**: The programming language for implementing the application logic and interacting with Qt's APIs.
- **Qt GUI Module**: Provides classes for drawing and image manipulation.
- **Qt Widgets or Qt Quick**: Choose the appropriate UI toolkit based on your design preferences. Qt Widgets offers a traditional desktop-oriented approach, while Qt Quick enables the creation of fluid and touch-friendly interfaces.

- **Third-Party Libraries (Optional)**: Consider using external libraries for advanced image processing algorithms or format support, depending on your project's specific needs.

Project Structure

We'll adopt a modular and organized project structure to facilitate code maintainability and extensibility. The project will likely comprise the following components:

- **Main Window**: The central window of the application, housing the UI elements and coordinating the overall functionality.
- **Image Canvas**: The area where the image is displayed and edited.
- **Editing Tools**: Individual components or modules for implementing specific editing functionalities, such as cropping, resizing, or applying filters.
- **UI Components**: Widgets or QML elements for constructing the user interface, including toolbars, menus, and property editors.

Development Approach

We'll adopt an iterative and incremental development approach, starting with basic image loading and display functionalities and gradually adding more advanced editing tools and features. We'll leverage Qt Creator's powerful IDE to design the UI, write C++ code, and debug the application throughout the development process.

Building a custom image editor is an exciting project that showcases the power and flexibility of Qt in the realm of graphics and UI development. By fulfilling the functional and non-functional requirements, leveraging Qt's graphics capabilities, and adopting a structured development approach, we'll create an image editor that empowers users to unleash their creativity and transform their images with ease and precision.

Image Manipulation with Qt

At the heart of our custom image editor lies the ability to manipulate and transform images, empowering users to unleash their creativity and achieve their desired visual effects. Qt's graphics framework provides a robust set of classes and functions for working with images, enabling you to load, display, modify, and save images in various formats. In this section, we'll delve into the intricacies of image manipulation with Qt, exploring the key classes, techniques, and considerations involved in implementing the core editing functionalities of our image editor.

The QImage Class: The Canvas of Pixels

The `QImage` class serves as the canvas for representing and manipulating images in Qt. It encapsulates the image data, including pixel values, color depth, and dimensions, providing a versatile interface for performing various image processing operations.

Loading Images

To load an image into your Qt application, you can utilize the `QImage` constructor or the `load()` function, specifying the file path or a byte array containing the image data. Qt supports various image formats, including JPEG, PNG, BMP, and GIF, allowing you to work with a wide range of image types.

C++

```
QImage image;
if (image.load("my_image.jpg")) {
    // Image loaded successfully
} else {
    // Handle loading error
```

}

In this example, we create a `QImage` object and attempt to load an image from the file "my_image.jpg." We then check the return value of the `load()` function to ensure the image was loaded successfully.

Displaying Images

Once you have a `QImage` object, you can display it within your GUI using a `QLabel` or by painting it directly onto a `QWidget` or `QGraphicsScene`.

C++

```
QLabel* imageLabel = new QLabel(this);
imageLabel->setPixmap(QPixmap::fromImage(image));
```

In this example, we create a `QLabel` and set its `pixmap` property to a `QPixmap` created from the

`QImage`. The image will then be displayed within the label widget.

Image Transformations

Qt's graphics framework provides a rich set of functions for performing various image transformations, enabling you to implement essential editing functionalities in your image editor. Some common transformations include:

- **Scaling and Resizing**: Adjust the dimensions of the image using the `scaled()` or `scaledToWidth()`/`scaledToHeight()` functions.
- **Cropping**: Extract a specific region of the image using the `copy()` function with rectangular coordinates.
- **Rotating**: Rotate the image by a specified angle using the `transformed()` function with a `QTransform` object.
- **Flipping**: Flip the image horizontally or vertically using the `mirrored()` function.

Color Adjustments and Filters

Qt's `QImage` class also provides methods for manipulating pixel values and applying color adjustments or filters to the image. You can adjust brightness, contrast, saturation, or hue, or apply more complex filters like grayscale, sepia, blur, or sharpen.

C++

```
QImage grayscaleImage = image.convertToFormat(QImage::Format_Grayscale8);
```

In this example, we convert the original image to grayscale using the `convertToFormat()` function.

Drawing and Annotations

To add text overlays, shapes, or other annotations to your image, you can utilize Qt's painting system. The `QPainter` class provides a powerful interface for drawing on a `QImage` or other paint devices.

C++

```
QPainter painter(&image);
painter.setPen(Qt::red);
```

```
painter.setFont(QFont("Arial", 20));
painter.drawText(10,    30,    "Hello,
Qt!");
```

In this example, we create a `QPainter` object and use it to draw red text with the Arial font on the image.

Saving Images

Once you've finished editing your image, you can save it to a file using the `save()` function, specifying the desired file path and format.

C++

```
if    (image.save("edited_image.png",
"PNG")) {
    // Image saved successfully
} else {
    // Handle saving error
}
```

In this example, we save the edited image in PNG format to the file "edited_image.png."

Performance Considerations

Image manipulation operations can be computationally intensive, especially for large or high-resolution images. To ensure a responsive user experience, consider the following performance optimization techniques:

- **Lazy Loading**: Load images only when they are needed, rather than upfront, to reduce memory consumption and startup time.
- **Caching**: Cache processed images or intermediate results to avoid redundant computations.
- **Multithreading**: Offload computationally expensive image processing tasks to separate threads to prevent blocking the main thread and maintain GUI responsiveness.

Qt's graphics framework provides a robust foundation for image manipulation, empowering you to implement essential editing functionalities in your custom image editor. By leveraging the `QImage` class, transformation functions, color adjustments, painting capabilities, and performance optimization techniques, you can create a powerful and versatile image editor that caters to the creative needs of your users.

Designing the Editor Interface

The interface of an image editor is the bridge between the user's creative intent and the powerful image manipulation capabilities at their disposal. A well-designed interface should be intuitive, visually appealing, and efficient, empowering users to navigate effortlessly through editing tools, access image properties, and preview their transformations in real-time. In this section, we'll embark on the design journey of our custom image editor's interface, exploring layout considerations, widget selection, and user experience principles that contribute to a seamless and productive editing environment.

Layout and Organization

The layout of our image editor's interface should prioritize clarity and accessibility, presenting tools and features in a logical and organized manner. We'll leverage Qt's layout managers to arrange widgets strategically, ensuring a balanced composition and adaptability to different screen sizes and resolutions.

A typical image editor interface might include the following sections:

- **Image Canvas**: The central focal point, displaying the image being edited and providing an interactive space for applying transformations and adjustments.
- **Toolbar or Ribbon**: A collection of icons or buttons representing various editing tools and functionalities, offering quick and convenient access to frequently used features.
- **Menu Bar**: A traditional menu structure for organizing and accessing additional commands, settings, and options.
- **Property Editor or Panel**: A dedicated area for displaying and modifying image properties, such as dimensions, resolution, color profiles, or layer information.
- **History or Layers Panel**: Provides a visual representation of the editing history or layers within the image, allowing users to undo or redo actions and manage composite images.

Widget Selection

Qt offers a rich selection of widgets that can be employed to construct the various sections of our image editor's interface. Here are some common choices:

- **Image Canvas**:
    - `QGraphicsView` (for a scalable and interactive canvas)
    - `QLabel` (for simpler image display)
- **Toolbar or Ribbon**:
    - `QToolBar` (for a traditional toolbar)
    - Custom widgets or QML elements (for a modern ribbon interface)
- **Menu Bar**:
    - `QMenuBar` (for creating the main menu structure)
    - `QMenu` and `QAction` (for defining menu items and actions)
- **Property Editor or Panel**:
    - `QGroupBox` or `QScrollArea` (for grouping and organizing properties)
    - `QLabel`, `QLineEdit`, `QSpinBox`, `QSlider`, etc. (for displaying and editing property values)
- **History or Layers Panel**:
    - `QListWidget` or `QTreeWidget` (for displaying a list or tree of editing history or layers)

User Experience Considerations

Designing an intuitive and user-friendly interface requires careful consideration of user experience principles. Strive for:

- **Clarity and Simplicity**: Present information and controls in a clear and concise manner, avoiding clutter and overwhelming the user.
- **Consistency**: Maintain consistency in visual style, terminology, and interaction patterns throughout the interface.
- **Discoverability**: Make tools and features easily discoverable through intuitive icons, labels, and tooltips.
- **Efficiency**: Provide shortcuts and streamlined workflows for common tasks, minimizing the number of clicks or steps required.
- **Feedback and Responsiveness**: Offer immediate visual feedback to user actions, such as highlighting selected areas or updating previews in real-time.

Prototyping and Iteration

Utilize Qt Designer's visual design capabilities to rapidly prototype different interface layouts and experiment with widget arrangements. Gather feedback from potential users and iterate on your design to ensure it meets their needs and expectations.

Designing the editor interface is a crucial step in creating a user-friendly and effective image editor. By carefully considering layout, widget selection, and user experience principles, we can craft an interface that empowers users to navigate effortlessly through editing tools, access image properties, and achieve their desired image transformations with ease and precision.

Implementing Editing Features

With a well-designed interface in place, it's time to breathe life into our custom image editor by implementing the core editing functionalities that empower users to transform and enhance their images. In this section, we'll delve into the implementation details of essential editing features, such as cropping, resizing, rotating, adjusting colors, applying filters, and adding text or annotations. We'll explore the techniques, algorithms, and Qt classes involved in bringing these features to life, ensuring our image editor provides a versatile and powerful toolkit for creative expression.

Cropping: Focusing on the Essentials

Cropping allows users to select a specific region of an image and discard the rest, focusing on the area of interest. To implement cropping in our image editor, we'll leverage Qt's `QImage::copy()` function, which extracts a rectangular region from an image.

C++

```
void      ImageEditor::cropImage(const QRect& cropRect) {
          QImage croppedImage = originalImage.copy(cropRect);
     // Display the cropped image or save it to a new file
}
```

In this example, the `cropImage()` function takes a `QRect` object representing the cropping rectangle and uses `QImage::copy()` to extract the corresponding region from the `originalImage`. The resulting `croppedImage` can then be displayed in the image canvas or saved to a new file.

Resizing: Adapting to Different Dimensions

Resizing enables users to adjust the dimensions of an image, making it suitable for various purposes or display constraints. Qt's `QImage::scaled()` function provides a convenient way to resize images, offering different scaling algorithms and options for maintaining aspect ratio or smooth scaling.

C++

```
void      ImageEditor::resizeImage(int newWidth, int newHeight) {
          QImage   resizedImage   = originalImage.scaled(newWidth, newHeight,       Qt::KeepAspectRatio, Qt::SmoothTransformation);
     // Display the resized image or save it to a new file
}
```

In this example, the `resizeImage()` function takes the desired new width and height and uses `QImage::scaled()` to resize the `originalImage`, preserving the aspect ratio and applying smooth scaling.

Rotating and Flipping: Changing Perspectives

Rotating and flipping images allow users to alter their orientation or perspective. Qt's `QImage::transformed()` function, in conjunction with `QTransform` objects, facilitates these transformations.

C++

```
void      ImageEditor::rotateImage(int angle) {
    QTransform transform;
    transform.rotate(angle);
        QImage   rotatedImage  = originalImage.transformed(transform);
    // Display the rotated image or save it to a new file
}

void      ImageEditor::flipImage(bool horizontal) {
```

```
    QImage    flippedImage    =
originalImage.mirrored(horizontal,
!horizontal);
    // Display the flipped image or
save it to a new file
}
```

In these examples, we use `QTransform` to define rotation and mirroring transformations and apply them to the `originalImage` using `QImage::transformed()` and `QImage::mirrored()`, respectively.

Color Adjustments: Fine-Tuning the Palette

Color adjustments empower users to enhance or modify the colors within an image. Qt's `QImage` class provides methods for pixel-level manipulation, allowing you to implement brightness, contrast, saturation, and hue adjustments.

C++

```
void ImageEditor::adjustBrightness(int value) {
```

```
    // Iterate over pixels and adjust
brightness based on 'value'
    // ...
}

void    ImageEditor::adjustContrast(int
value) {
    // Iterate over pixels and adjust
contrast based on 'value'
    // ...
}

//   ...   similar   functions   for
saturation and hue adjustments
```

In these examples, we outline the basic structure of functions for adjusting brightness and contrast. The actual implementation would involve iterating over the image pixels and modifying their values based on the provided adjustment value.

Filters and Effects: Creative Transformations

Filters and effects add a touch of artistic flair to images, enabling users to apply various visual transformations. Qt's graphics framework, along with potential third-party libraries, provides a plethora of options for implementing filters like grayscale, sepia, blur, sharpen, and many more.

C++

```
void ImageEditor::applyGrayscaleFilter() {
        QImage grayscaleImage = originalImage.convertToFormat(QImage::Format_Grayscale8);
    // Display the grayscale image or save it to a new file
}

void ImageEditor::applyBlurFilter(int radius) {
    // Apply blur filter using Qt's image processing functions or external library
    // ...
}

// ... similar functions for other filters and effects
```

In these examples, we demonstrate the application of a grayscale filter using `QImage::convertToFormat()` and outline the structure of a function for applying a blur filter, potentially utilizing Qt's built-in image processing capabilities or an external library.

Text and Annotations: Adding Context

Text overlays and annotations provide context and additional information to images. Qt's painting system, with the `QPainter` class, enables you to draw text, shapes, lines, and arrows directly onto the image.

C++

```
void       ImageEditor::addText(const QString& text, const QFont& font, const QColor& color, const QPoint& position) {
    QPainter painter(&image);
    painter.setPen(color);
    painter.setFont(font);
    painter.drawText(position, text);
    // Display the annotated image or save it to a new file
}
```

In this example, we use `QPainter` to draw text on the image, specifying the text content, font, color, and position.

Implementing editing features is where the true magic of our custom image editor comes to life. By leveraging Qt's image manipulation capabilities, painting system, and potential third-party libraries, we can empower users to crop, resize, rotate, adjust colors, apply filters, and add text or annotations to their images, unleashing their creativity and transforming their visual creations with ease and precision.

Chapter 16: Creating a Networked Chat Application

Project Overview and Requirements

In the realm of modern communication, where real-time interaction and seamless connectivity are paramount, chat applications have become an indispensable tool for connecting individuals and communities across the globe. In this chapter, we embark on an exciting project to build a networked chat application using the power of Qt and C++. By leveraging Qt's networking capabilities and intuitive UI framework, we'll craft a chat application that enables users to exchange messages, share files, and engage in real-time conversations, fostering a sense of community and connection in the digital age.

Project Goals

Our primary goal is to develop a chat application that facilitates seamless communication between multiple users over a network. The application should provide a user-friendly interface for sending and receiving messages, support basic chat features like group chats and private messaging, and ensure secure and reliable message transmission.

Functional Requirements

Let's outline the core functionalities that our networked chat application should encompass:

- **User Authentication and Registration**:
    - Allow users to create accounts and log in securely.
    - Implement password hashing and salting for enhanced security.
    - Optionally, provide social login integration (e.g., Google, Facebook).
- **Real-time Messaging**:
    - Enable users to send and receive text messages in real-time.
    - Support for group chats and private messaging.
    - Display timestamps and user avatars for each message.
    - Optionally, implement message editing and deletion.
- **File Sharing**:
    - Allow users to share files (e.g., images, documents, videos) with each other.

- Provide progress indicators for file uploads and downloads.
- Implement mechanisms for handling large file transfers efficiently.
- **User Presence and Status**:
    - Display online/offline status for each user.
    - Optionally, implement typing indicators or "last seen" timestamps.
- **User Interface**:
    - Intuitive and visually appealing interface.
    - Clear separation of chat rooms, user lists, and message areas.
    - Support for emoticons or custom emojis.
    - Customizable themes or skins.

Non-functional Requirements

In addition to functional requirements, let's consider some important non-functional aspects:

- **Performance**: The chat application should handle message and file transfers efficiently, even with a large number of concurrent users.

- **Scalability**: The architecture should be designed to accommodate future growth and increasing user loads.
- **Security**: Implement appropriate security measures to protect user data and prevent unauthorized access or malicious activities.
- **Reliability**: Ensure message delivery and data integrity, even in the face of network disruptions or errors.
- **Usability**: The interface should be user-friendly and easy to navigate, catering to users of varying technical expertise.

Technology Stack

We'll leverage the following technologies to build our networked chat application:

- **Qt 6**: The core framework for GUI development, networking, and cross-platform compatibility.
- **C++**: The programming language for implementing the application logic and interacting with Qt's APIs.
- **Qt Network Module**: Provides classes for TCP and UDP communication, enabling real-time message and file transfers.
- **Qt Widgets or Qt Quick**: Choose the appropriate UI toolkit based on your design

preferences. Qt Widgets offers a traditional desktop-oriented approach, while Qt Quick enables the creation of fluid and touch-friendly interfaces.
- **Third-Party Libraries (Optional)**: Consider using external libraries for encryption, database integration, or other specialized functionalities, depending on your project's specific needs.

Project Structure

We'll adopt a modular and organized project structure to facilitate code maintainability and scalability. The project will likely comprise the following components:

- **Client Application**: The frontend application that users interact with, responsible for UI rendering, message composition, and network communication.
- **Server Application (Optional)**: A backend server that handles user authentication, message routing, and potentially data storage.
- **Network Communication Module**: Handles the low-level TCP or UDP communication, serialization and deserialization of messages, and error handling.

- **UI Components**: Widgets or QML elements for constructing the user interface, including chat windows, user lists, message displays, and file transfer components.

Development Approach

We'll adopt an iterative and incremental development approach, starting with basic client-server communication and gradually adding more advanced features like group chats, file sharing, and user presence. We'll leverage Qt Creator's powerful IDE to design the UI, write C++ code, and debug the application throughout the development process.

Building a networked chat application is a challenging yet rewarding project that showcases the power of Qt in facilitating real-time communication and collaboration. By adhering to the functional and non-functional requirements, leveraging Qt's networking capabilities, and adopting a structured development approach, we'll create a chat application that fosters connection, engagement, and community in the digital age.

Client-Server Architecture

In the realm of networked applications, the client-server architecture stands as a cornerstone, providing a robust and scalable foundation for communication and data exchange. This architectural pattern involves a clear separation of concerns, where clients initiate requests to a central server, which processes these requests and sends back corresponding responses. In the context of our networked chat application, the client-server architecture enables us to centralize critical functionalities, such as user authentication, message routing, and potentially data storage, while empowering multiple clients to connect, communicate, and collaborate seamlessly. In this section, we'll delve into the intricacies of the client-server architecture, exploring its components, communication flow, and advantages in building a scalable and efficient chat application.

The Client: The User's Gateway

The client application serves as the user's gateway to the chat system, providing the graphical user interface (GUI) through which users interact with the application. It is responsible for rendering chat windows, displaying user lists, presenting messages, and handling user input, such as composing and sending messages or initiating file transfers.

The client communicates with the server using network protocols like TCP or UDP, sending requests and receiving responses in a structured and synchronized manner. It handles the serialization and deserialization of messages, ensuring that data is transmitted and interpreted correctly between the client and server.

The Server: The Central Hub

The server application acts as the central hub of the chat system, receiving requests from multiple clients, processing them, and dispatching appropriate responses. It manages user authentication, maintains a list of connected users, routes messages between clients, and potentially stores chat history or other relevant data.

The server employs network protocols to listen for incoming connections from clients, accept those connections, and establish communication channels. It handles the concurrent processing of multiple client requests, ensuring efficient and timely responses.

Communication Flow

The communication flow in a client-server architecture typically follows these steps:

1. **Client Connection**: A client initiates a connection to the server, providing necessary authentication credentials if required.
2. **Server Acceptance**: The server accepts the client's connection, establishes a communication channel, and adds the client to its list of connected users.
3. **Client Requests**: The client sends requests to the server, such as sending a message, requesting a file transfer, or updating its presence status.
4. **Server Processing**: The server receives the client's request, processes it according to the application's logic, and prepares a corresponding response.
5. **Server Response**: The server sends the response back to the client, containing the requested data or an acknowledgment of the action.
6. **Client Handling**: The client receives the server's response, deserializes the data, and updates its UI or performs other actions as needed.

Advantages of Client-Server Architecture

The client-server architecture offers several advantages for building networked chat applications:

- **Centralized Control**: Centralizing critical functionalities on the server simplifies management, maintenance, and updates.
- **Scalability**: The server can handle multiple concurrent client connections, enabling the chat application to scale to a large number of users.
- **Data Persistence**: The server can store chat history, user profiles, and other data, ensuring persistence and accessibility even when clients disconnect.
- **Security**: The server can implement authentication, authorization, and encryption mechanisms to protect user data and prevent unauthorized access.
- **Load Balancing**: Multiple servers can be deployed to distribute the workload and handle high traffic volumes.

The client-server architecture provides a robust and scalable foundation for building networked chat applications. By clearly separating the concerns of the client and server, centralizing critical functionalities, and leveraging Qt's networking capabilities, you can create a chat system that fosters seamless communication, collaboration, and community among its users.

Implementing Chat Functionality

The core essence of a chat application lies in its ability to facilitate real-time communication between users. This involves the seamless exchange of messages, notifications of user presence, and potentially the sharing of files or other media. In this section, we'll delve into the implementation details of the chat functionality within our Qt-based application, exploring the techniques and considerations involved in crafting a responsive, interactive, and engaging chat experience.

Message Exchange: The Heartbeat of Communication

At the heart of our chat application lies the exchange of messages between users. We'll leverage Qt's networking capabilities, specifically TCP or UDP communication, to transmit and receive messages in real-time.

- **Message Structure**: Define a clear and concise message structure that

encapsulates the essential information, such as the sender, recipient(s), timestamp, and message content. Consider using a serialization format like JSON or Protocol Buffers for efficient and platform-independent data exchange.
- **Client-Side Handling**: On the client-side, implement mechanisms for composing and sending messages. This might involve text input fields, emoji pickers, or even voice-to-text functionality. Once a message is composed, serialize it into the defined message structure and transmit it to the server using the appropriate network protocol.
- **Server-Side Routing**: On the server-side, receive incoming messages from clients, deserialize them, and route them to the intended recipients. This might involve maintaining a list of connected users, identifying the target recipients based on the message structure, and forwarding the message to their respective connections.
- **Client-Side Display**: Upon receiving a message from the server, the client deserializes it, extracts the relevant information, and displays it in the chat window. Consider using a `QListWidget` or

a custom QML component to present messages in an organized and visually appealing manner, incorporating timestamps and user avatars for context.

User Presence and Status

Informing users about the online/offline status of their contacts enhances the chat experience and facilitates real-time communication. We'll implement mechanisms to track and display user presence information.

- **Server-Side Tracking**: The server maintains a list of connected users and their current status (online, offline, away). When a user connects or disconnects, the server updates its internal list and broadcasts notifications to other connected users.
- **Client-Side Updates**: Clients receive presence updates from the server and update their user lists accordingly. Consider using visual cues, such as colored indicators or icons, to represent user status clearly.
- **Typing Indicators (Optional)**: To further enhance the real-time experience, you can implement typing indicators that visually inform users when others are actively

composing a message. This involves sending periodic updates from the client to the server, which then broadcasts these notifications to the relevant recipients.

Group Chats and Private Messaging

Beyond one-on-one conversations, our chat application should support group chats and private messaging, catering to diverse communication needs.

- **Group Chat Management**: Implement mechanisms for creating, joining, and leaving group chats. The server maintains a list of active group chats and their participants, facilitating message routing and user management within each group.
- **Private Messaging**: Enable users to initiate private conversations with specific individuals. The server ensures that messages intended for private chats are delivered only to the designated recipients, maintaining privacy and confidentiality.

File Sharing

File sharing adds another layer of richness to chat interactions, allowing users to exchange images, documents, and other media. We'll integrate file transfer capabilities into our application, ensuring efficient and reliable file transmission.

- **File Transfer Protocol**: Choose an appropriate file transfer protocol, such as FTP or a custom protocol built on TCP, to handle file uploads and downloads.
- **Progress Indication**: Provide visual feedback to users during file transfers, displaying progress bars or percentage indicators to keep them informed about the transfer status.
- **Error Handling**: Implement robust error handling mechanisms to gracefully manage file transfer failures, network disruptions, or other issues that might arise during the process.

Implementing chat functionality is the heart and soul of building a networked chat application. By leveraging Qt's networking capabilities, designing efficient message exchange mechanisms, handling user presence and status, supporting group chats and private messaging, and integrating file-sharing features, you can create a chat experience that fosters real-time communication, collaboration, and community building.

Handling User Authentication

In the realm of networked applications, where user identity and data security are paramount, user authentication emerges as a critical component. It serves as the gatekeeper, ensuring that only authorized individuals can access and interact with the system. In the context of our chat application, user authentication safeguards user accounts, protects sensitive information, and maintains the integrity of communication channels. In this section, we'll delve into the intricacies of handling user authentication in Qt, exploring techniques for secure login, registration, and session management, empowering you to build a chat application that prioritizes user privacy and data protection.

Secure Login and Registration

The foundation of user authentication lies in secure login and registration processes. Let's explore the key considerations:

- **User Credentials**: Capture user credentials, typically a username and password, through secure input fields in your GUI. Consider using `QLineEdit` with password masking to protect sensitive information.

- **Password Hashing and Salting**: Never store passwords in plain text. Employ robust hashing algorithms like bcrypt or Argon2 to convert passwords into irreversible hashes. Additionally, use unique salts for each user to further enhance security and protect against rainbow table attacks.
- **Server-Side Validation**: Upon login, transmit the entered username and password hash to the server for validation. The server compares the received hash with the stored hash for the given username, granting access only if they match.
- **Registration Process**: Implement a registration process that allows new users to create accounts. Capture necessary information, such as username, password, and potentially email address or other profile details. Validate the input to ensure it meets your application's requirements and store the user's information securely on the server, including the hashed and salted password.
- **Session Management**: Upon successful login, generate a unique session identifier or token for the user. Store this token securely on both the client and server, associating it with the user's session. Include this token in subsequent requests from the client to the

server to maintain authentication and authorization throughout the user's interaction with the application.

Enhancing Security

Beyond basic login and registration, consider implementing additional security measures to fortify your chat application:

- **Two-Factor Authentication (2FA)**: Add an extra layer of security by requiring users to provide a second authentication factor, such as a code generated by an authenticator app or sent via SMS, in addition to their password.
- **Password Strength Enforcement**: Enforce strong password policies, requiring users to create passwords that meet specific complexity criteria, such as minimum length, inclusion of uppercase and lowercase letters, numbers, and special characters.
- **Account Lockout**: Implement mechanisms to temporarily lock user accounts after a certain number of failed login attempts, mitigating brute-force attacks.
- **Secure Communication**: Utilize secure protocols like HTTPS or encrypt sensitive

data transmitted between the client and server to protect against eavesdropping or tampering.

Qt's Network Authentication Support

Qt's Network module provides built-in support for various authentication mechanisms, simplifying the implementation of secure login and session management. The `QNetworkAccessManager` class can handle authentication challenges from the server, prompting the user for credentials or utilizing stored credentials to authenticate requests.

Handling user authentication is a critical aspect of building secure and trustworthy networked chat applications. By implementing robust login and registration processes, employing password hashing and salting, managing sessions effectively, and considering additional security measures, you can create a chat application that prioritizes user privacy, data protection, and the integrity of communication channels.

Part V: Best Practices and Beyond

Chapter 17: Coding Standards and Design Patterns

Qt Coding Conventions

In the realm of software development, where collaboration, maintainability, and readability are paramount, coding conventions emerge as the guiding principles that ensure consistency and clarity throughout your codebase. Qt, with its extensive framework and vast community of developers, has established a set of coding conventions that foster a shared understanding and streamline the development process. In this section, we'll delve into the essence of Qt coding conventions, exploring their rationale, key principles, and practical applications in crafting clean, elegant, and maintainable Qt code.

The Rationale Behind Coding Conventions

Coding conventions, while seemingly trivial, play a crucial role in promoting code quality and facilitating collaboration. By adhering to a set of established guidelines, you can:

- **Enhance Readability:** Consistent formatting, naming conventions, and code structure improve code readability, making it

easier for others (and yourself) to understand and navigate your codebase.
- **Reduce Errors:** Clear and well-structured code minimizes the likelihood of errors and facilitates debugging, leading to more robust and reliable applications.
- **Facilitate Collaboration:** When multiple developers work on the same project, coding conventions ensure a shared understanding of the code, enabling seamless collaboration and reducing friction.
- **Streamline Maintenance:** Well-organized and consistently formatted code is easier to maintain and update, reducing the effort required for future enhancements or bug fixes.

Key Principles of Qt Coding Conventions

Qt's coding conventions encompass a range of guidelines that cover various aspects of code formatting, naming, and structure. Let's explore some of the key principles:

- **Naming Conventions**:
    - **Classes**: Class names should start with an uppercase letter and use

camel case (e.g., `MyClass`, `NetworkManager`).
- **Functions and Methods**: Function and method names should start with a lowercase letter and use camel case (e.g., `calculateSum`, `openConnection`).
- **Variables**: Variable names should start with a lowercase letter and use camel case (e.g., `counter`, `userName`).
- **Constants**: Constant names should be in all uppercase letters with underscores separating words (e.g., `MAX_VALUE`, `DEFAULT_PORT`).

- **Indentation and Spacing**:
  - Use four spaces for indentation.
  - Place spaces around operators and after commas.
  - Use blank lines to separate logical blocks of code.
- **Braces and Control Structures**:
  - Place opening braces on the same line as the control structure keyword (e.g., `if`, `for`, `while`).

- Place closing braces on their own line, aligned with the corresponding control structure keyword.
- Use braces even for single-statement blocks to enhance readability and prevent potential errors.
- **Comments**:
    - Use `//` for single-line comments and `/* ... */` for multi-line comments.
    - Write clear and concise comments that explain the purpose and intent of your code.
    - Avoid commenting on obvious or self-explanatory code.
- **Qt-Specific Conventions**:
    - **Signals and Slots**: Signal names should start with a lowercase letter and use camel case (e.g., `valueChanged`, `buttonClicked`). Slot names should follow the same convention as regular member functions.
    - **QML**: Adhere to QML's coding conventions, which include guidelines for element naming, property declarations, and JavaScript code formatting.

Practical Applications

Let's illustrate the application of Qt coding conventions with a code example:

C++

```
class MyNetworkManager : public QObject
{
    Q_OBJECT

public:
    explicit MyNetworkManager(QObject *parent = nullptr);
    ~MyNetworkManager();

    Q_INVOKABLE void sendRequest(const QString &url);

signals:
    void requestCompleted(const QByteArray &data);
    void requestFailed(const QString &errorMessage);

private:
    QNetworkAccessManager *m_networkManager;
```

```
};
```

In this example, we adhere to Qt's naming conventions for the class name (`MyNetworkManager`), function name (`sendRequest`), signal names (`requestCompleted`, `requestFailed`), and member variable name (`m_networkManager`). We also use proper indentation, spacing, and brace placement to enhance code readability.

Tools and Automation

Qt Creator, the integrated development environment for Qt, provides built-in support for code formatting and style checking. You can configure Qt Creator to automatically format your code according to Qt's coding conventions, ensuring consistency and saving you valuable time.

Additionally, tools like `clang-format` or `Artistic Style` can be integrated into your development workflow to automate code formatting and enforce coding standards across your entire project.

Qt coding conventions are more than just arbitrary rules; they are guiding principles that foster code quality, readability, and maintainability. By adhering to these conventions, you contribute to a shared understanding within the Qt community, streamline collaboration, and ensure that your codebase remains clean, elegant, and adaptable for future enhancements.

Design Patterns for Qt Development

In the realm of software development, where complexity and scalability are constant challenges, design patterns emerge as time-tested solutions to recurring problems. These patterns, distilled from the collective experience of countless developers, offer reusable blueprints for structuring your code, promoting maintainability, and fostering flexibility. Qt, with its rich object-oriented framework and event-driven architecture, provides a fertile ground for applying design patterns to streamline development and enhance code quality. In this section, we'll explore some of the most commonly used design patterns in Qt development, unraveling their essence, applications, and the benefits they bring to your projects.

Model-View-Controller (MVC)

The Model-View-Controller (MVC) pattern stands as a cornerstone of GUI development, providing a clear separation of concerns between data management (model), data presentation (view), and user interaction (controller). In Qt, this pattern manifests through the Model-View architecture, where models encapsulate data, views render the data, and delegates control the interaction and presentation of individual data items.

By adopting the MVC pattern, you can achieve:

- **Data Independence**: Decouple your data from its visual representation, enabling you to modify the presentation without affecting the underlying data structure.
- **Multiple Views**: Connect a single model to multiple views, each presenting the data in a different way, fostering flexibility and adaptability.
- **Code Reusability**: Separate the logic for data handling, presentation, and interaction into distinct components, promoting code reuse and maintainability.

Signals and Slots: The Observer Pattern in Action

Qt's signal-slot mechanism embodies the Observer pattern, where objects can register their interest in specific events or state changes and receive notifications when those events occur. This decoupled communication model fosters loose coupling between objects, enhancing modularity and flexibility.

By utilizing signals and slots, you can:

- **Decouple Objects**: Objects can communicate indirectly through signals and slots, reducing dependencies and promoting code reusability.
- **Handle Events Dynamically**: Respond to events and user interactions in a flexible and adaptable manner, triggering actions or updating the UI as needed.
- **Build Reactive Systems**: Create UIs that react automatically to data changes or other events, providing a seamless and interactive user experience.

Singleton Pattern: Ensuring Unique Access

The Singleton pattern ensures that a class has only one instance and provides a global point of access to it. This is useful for managing resources or services that should exist in a single instance throughout your application's lifetime.

In Qt, you can implement the Singleton pattern using a static member function that returns a pointer to the single instance of the class.

C++

```
class MySingleton : public QObject
{
    Q_OBJECT

public:
    static MySingleton* instance()
    {
        static MySingleton* s_instance = new MySingleton;
        return s_instance;
    }

private:
    explicit MySingleton(QObject *parent = nullptr);
    ~MySingleton();
};
```

In this example, the `instance()` function ensures that only one instance of `MySingleton` is created and provides access to it throughout the application.

Other Design Patterns

Qt's rich ecosystem and object-oriented nature make it conducive to applying various other design patterns, including:

- **Factory Method**: Creates objects without specifying their concrete classes, promoting flexibility and extensibility.
- **Abstract Factory**: Provides an interface for creating families of related or dependent objects without specifying their concrete classes.
- **Strategy Pattern**: Defines a family of algorithms, encapsulates each one, and makes them interchangeable, allowing the algorithm to vary independently from the clients that use it.
- **Decorator Pattern**: Attaches additional responsibilities to an object dynamically, providing a flexible alternative to subclassing for extending functionality.

Choosing the Right Pattern

Selecting the appropriate design pattern depends on the specific problem you're trying to solve and the architectural constraints of your application. Consider the following factors:

- **Problem Domain**: Identify the recurring problem or challenge you're facing in your code.
- **Flexibility and Extensibility**: Choose patterns that promote flexibility and allow for future enhancements or modifications.
- **Maintainability**: Select patterns that enhance code readability, organization, and maintainability.
- **Performance**: Consider the performance implications of different patterns, especially in critical sections of your application.

Design patterns are invaluable tools in the Qt developer's arsenal, offering proven solutions to recurring problems and promoting code quality, maintainability, and flexibility. By understanding the essence of these patterns and their applications in Qt development, you can structure your code effectively, enhance collaboration, and build robust and scalable applications that stand the test of time.

Writing Clean and Maintainable Code

In the ever-evolving landscape of software development, where projects grow in complexity and teams collaborate across time and space, the importance of writing clean and maintainable code cannot be overstated. Clean code is not merely a matter of aesthetics; it's a testament to your craftsmanship, a reflection of your commitment to quality, and a key factor in the long-term success of your Qt projects. In this section, we'll delve into the art of writing clean and maintainable code in Qt, exploring principles, practices, and techniques that empower you to create codebases that are not only functional but also easy to understand, modify, and extend.

The Essence of Clean Code

Clean code is characterized by its clarity, simplicity, and elegance. It's code that is easy to read, understand, and reason about, even for developers who didn't write it. It's code that is well-organized, modular, and adheres to established conventions, minimizing the cognitive load required to comprehend its intricacies. Clean code is a joy to work with, fostering productivity, collaboration, and a sense of pride in your craft.

Principles of Clean Code

Let's explore some of the key principles that underpin the practice of writing clean code:

- **Meaningful Names**: Choose names for variables, functions, classes, and other identifiers that accurately reflect their purpose and intent. Avoid cryptic abbreviations or single-letter variables that obscure meaning.
- **Clear and Concise Functions**: Keep functions short and focused, performing a single, well-defined task. Break down complex logic into smaller, more manageable functions that are easier to understand and test.
- **Consistent Formatting**: Adhere to Qt's coding conventions or establish your own consistent formatting style. Consistent indentation, spacing, and brace placement enhance readability and reduce cognitive friction.
- **Meaningful Comments**: Use comments to explain the *why* behind your code, not just the *what*. Focus on providing context, clarifying intentions, and documenting non-obvious or complex logic.

- **Error Handling**: Anticipate and handle potential errors gracefully, providing informative feedback to the user and preventing crashes. Employ clear and descriptive error messages that guide users in resolving issues.
- **Modularity and Reusability**: Break down your code into modular components that encapsulate specific functionalities. Design these components to be reusable across different parts of your application or even in other projects.
- **Testability**: Write code that is easy to test, with clear separation of concerns and well-defined interfaces. Unit tests and integration tests help ensure the correctness and reliability of your code.

Practical Tips for Clean Qt Code

Let's delve into some practical tips specific to Qt development:

- **Leverage Qt's Signal-Slot Mechanism**: Embrace Qt's signal-slot mechanism for communication between objects, promoting loose coupling and modularity.

- **Use Qt's Layouts Effectively**: Organize your widgets with Qt's layout managers to create responsive and visually pleasing interfaces.
- **Employ Qt's Style Sheets**: Customize the appearance of your widgets using Qt style sheets, ensuring a consistent and visually appealing look and feel.
- **Embrace Qt's Cross-Platform Philosophy**: Write code that is portable across different operating systems, minimizing platform-specific dependencies and maximizing code reuse.
- **Stay Updated with Qt's Best Practices**: Qt's ecosystem and best practices continue to evolve. Stay informed about the latest recommendations and guidelines to ensure your code remains modern and maintainable.

Tools for Code Quality

Qt Creator, the integrated development environment for Qt, provides several tools that aid in writing clean and maintainable code:

- **Code Formatting**: Configure Qt Creator to automatically format your code according to

Qt's coding conventions or your own custom style.
- **Code Refactoring**: Utilize Qt Creator's refactoring tools to rename identifiers, extract methods, or perform other code transformations that improve clarity and maintainability.
- **Static Code Analysis**: Integrate static code analysis tools like `clang-tidy` or `Cppcheck` into your workflow to identify potential errors, style violations, or performance bottlenecks early in the development process.

Writing clean and maintainable code is a journey, not a destination. It requires continuous effort, attention to detail, and a commitment to excellence. By embracing the principles of clean code, adhering to Qt's coding conventions, and leveraging the available tools, you can create Qt applications that are not only functional but also a pleasure to work with, fostering collaboration, maintainability, and long-term success.

Chapter 18: Troubleshooting and Debugging

Common Qt Errors

In the intricate world of Qt development, encountering errors is an inevitable part of the journey. From elusive compilation issues to perplexing runtime crashes, these obstacles can test your patience and impede your progress. However, armed with knowledge and a systematic approach, you can effectively troubleshoot and overcome these challenges, ensuring the smooth execution and stability of your Qt applications. In this section, we'll delve into some of the most common Qt errors, providing insights into their causes, symptoms, and practical solutions, empowering you to navigate the debugging landscape with confidence and efficiency.

Compilation Errors: Unraveling the Compiler's Cryptic Messages

Compilation errors, often manifested as a cascade of red text in Qt Creator's "Issues" pane, can be daunting at first glance. However, they provide crucial clues to pinpoint the root causes of issues within your code. Let's explore some common culprits:

- **Syntax Errors:** These errors arise from violations of C++ or QML syntax rules, such as missing semicolons, mismatched parentheses, or incorrect variable declarations. Qt Creator's code editor often underlines these errors in real-time, providing immediate feedback and facilitating quick fixes.
- **Linker Errors:** Linker errors occur during the linking stage, where the compiled object files are combined into an executable. These errors often stem from missing libraries, unresolved symbols, or conflicts between different versions of libraries. Ensure that all required Qt modules and external libraries are included in your project's `.pro` file and that their paths are correctly configured.
- **Header File Inclusion Issues**: Qt relies heavily on header files to define classes, functions, and other components. If header files are not included correctly or in the proper order, compilation errors can ensue. Double-check your `#include` directives, ensuring they reference the correct header files and are placed in the appropriate locations within your code.
- **Moc-Related Errors**: Qt's Meta-Object Compiler (MOC) generates additional code

to support signals, slots, and other meta-object features. If the MOC encounters issues processing your code, it might generate errors related to missing `Q_OBJECT` macros, incorrect signal or slot declarations, or conflicts with other meta-object systems. Ensure that your classes that utilize signals and slots inherit from `QObject` and include the `Q_OBJECT` macro in their declarations.

Runtime Errors: Taming Unexpected Behavior

Runtime errors, often manifesting as crashes or unexpected behavior during the execution of your application, can be particularly challenging to diagnose and resolve. However, Qt provides powerful debugging tools and techniques to help you identify and rectify these issues. Let's explore some common runtime errors:

- **Null Pointer Dereferencing**: Accessing a null pointer, a pointer that doesn't point to a valid memory location, triggers a runtime error. This often occurs when you forget to initialize a pointer or when an object is deleted prematurely. Use Qt Creator's debugger to inspect pointer values and track

their lifecycle to identify the source of the null pointer.
- **Memory Leaks**: Memory leaks occur when dynamically allocated memory is not properly deallocated, leading to a gradual accumulation of unused memory and potential performance degradation or crashes. Employ tools like Valgrind or Qt's built-in memory profiler to detect memory leaks and identify the code sections responsible for them. Embrace smart pointers to automate memory management and minimize the risk of leaks.
- **Out-of-Bounds Access**: Accessing elements of an array or container beyond their valid bounds triggers a runtime error. This often happens due to incorrect loop conditions, off-by-one errors, or improper handling of user input. Use Qt Creator's debugger to step through your code, inspect array or container sizes, and verify that your access patterns are within valid bounds.
- **Threading Issues**: Multithreaded applications are susceptible to race conditions, deadlocks, and other synchronization-related errors. These errors can be particularly elusive, as their occurrence might depend on specific thread

interleavings or timing conditions. Employ Qt's threading support and synchronization primitives carefully, adhere to best practices, and utilize debugging tools to identify and resolve threading issues.

General Troubleshooting Tips

In addition to the specific error types mentioned above, consider these general troubleshooting tips when encountering issues in your Qt applications:

- **Read the Error Messages Carefully**: Error messages, while sometimes cryptic, often provide valuable clues about the nature and location of the problem. Pay attention to the error code, file name, and line number mentioned in the message.
- **Consult the Qt Documentation**: Qt's comprehensive documentation is an invaluable resource for understanding classes, functions, and error codes. Refer to the documentation to gain insights into the expected behavior and potential pitfalls of specific Qt components.
- **Utilize Qt Creator's Debugging Tools**: Qt Creator offers a powerful debugger that allows you to step through your code,

inspect variables, set breakpoints, and analyze the call stack. Leverage these tools to pinpoint the exact location and cause of runtime errors.
- **Search Online Resources and Forums**: The Qt community is vast and supportive. Search online forums, Q&A sites, or Qt's official bug tracker to see if others have encountered similar issues and discovered solutions.
- **Isolate the Problem**: If your application is complex, try to isolate the problematic code section by commenting out parts of your code or creating minimal test cases that reproduce the error.
- **Seek Help**: If you're unable to resolve an error on your own, don't hesitate to seek help from the Qt community or consult with experienced Qt developers.

Encountering errors is an inevitable part of the Qt development process. However, armed with knowledge, a systematic approach, and the right tools, you can effectively troubleshoot and overcome these challenges. By understanding common Qt errors, their causes, and their solutions, you can navigate the debugging landscape with confidence and ensure the smooth execution and stability of your applications. Remember, every error is an opportunity to learn and grow as a Qt developer. Embrace the challenges, persevere through the debugging process, and emerge with a deeper understanding of Qt's intricacies and a refined skillset for building robust and reliable applications.

Debugging Techniques

In the intricate dance of software development, where bugs and unexpected behavior can lurk in the shadows, debugging emerges as an indispensable skill for any Qt developer. It's the art of systematically identifying, isolating, and resolving issues within your code, ensuring the smooth execution and reliability of your applications. Qt Creator, the powerful integrated development environment for Qt, provides a robust suite of debugging tools and techniques that empower you to navigate the debugging landscape with precision and efficiency. In this section, we'll delve into the essential debugging techniques in Qt Creator, equipping you with the knowledge and strategies to conquer bugs and deliver polished, high-quality applications.

Breakpoints: Pausing the Execution

Breakpoints are the strategic pauses you insert into your code, allowing you to examine the state of your application at specific points during its execution. By setting breakpoints at critical junctures, you can inspect variable values, step through the code line by line, and observe the flow of execution, gaining valuable insights into the inner workings of your application.

In Qt Creator, you can set breakpoints by clicking on the left margin next to the desired line of code. A red circle will appear, indicating the breakpoint. When you run your application in debug mode, the execution will pause at each breakpoint, allowing you to analyze the current state and identify potential issues.

Stepping Through Code: Navigating the Execution Flow

Once your application is paused at a breakpoint, you can use Qt Creator's stepping commands to navigate through the code execution:

- **Step Over**: Executes the current line of code and advances to the next line, skipping over any function calls.

- **Step Into**: Enters the function call on the current line and pauses at its first executable line.
- **Step Out**: Continues execution until the current function returns and pauses at the calling line.

By strategically stepping through your code, you can observe how variables change, track the flow of control, and pinpoint the exact location where an error or unexpected behavior occurs.

Inspecting Variables: Unveiling the Data

Qt Creator's debugger allows you to inspect the values of variables at any point during the execution. This invaluable feature empowers you to monitor data changes, identify incorrect values, and track down the root causes of bugs.

You can inspect variables by hovering over them in the code editor or by adding them to the "Locals and Expressions" view. The debugger displays the current value of each variable, along with its type and scope, providing crucial information for your debugging efforts.

Watching Expressions: Monitoring Dynamic Values

In addition to inspecting individual variables, you can also define watch expressions to monitor the values of complex expressions or combinations of variables. This allows you to track how specific values change throughout the execution, even if they are not directly assigned to variables.

To add a watch expression, navigate to the "Locals and Expressions" view, right-click, and choose "Add Expression." Enter the desired expression, and the debugger will evaluate it and display its value at each breakpoint or step.

Analyzing the Call Stack: Tracing the Execution Path

The call stack provides a historical record of function calls leading up to the current point of execution. By examining the call stack, you can trace the path your application took to reach a particular line of code, identify the functions involved, and pinpoint the source of an error or unexpected behavior.

Qt Creator's debugger displays the call stack in the "Stack" view, listing the function calls in reverse chronological order, with the most recent call at the top. You can click on any function in the call stack to jump to its corresponding source code and inspect its local variables.

Debugging Tips and Tricks

In addition to the core debugging techniques mentioned above, consider these additional tips and tricks:

- **Logging**: Strategically insert `qDebug()` statements or utilize a logging framework to print messages or variable values to the console, providing additional insights into your application's behavior.
- **Assertions**: Use `Q_ASSERT` macros to enforce assumptions about your code and catch potential errors early in the development process.
- **Conditional Breakpoints**: Set breakpoints that trigger only when specific conditions are met, allowing you to focus on specific scenarios or edge cases.
- **Remote Debugging**: Debug your application running on a remote device or embedded system using Qt Creator's remote debugging capabilities.

Debugging is an essential skill for any Qt developer, empowering you to identify, isolate, and resolve issues within your code. Qt Creator's robust debugging tools, including breakpoints, stepping commands, variable inspection, watch expressions, and call stack analysis, provide a comprehensive toolkit for navigating the debugging landscape with precision and efficiency.

Qt Test Framework

In the pursuit of software quality and reliability, testing emerges as an indispensable practice that ensures your Qt applications function as intended, even in the face of unexpected inputs or edge cases. Qt's Test framework provides a robust and integrated solution for creating and executing unit tests, enabling you to automate the verification of individual components and functionalities within your codebase. In this section, we'll delve into the essence of the Qt Test framework, exploring its core components, test creation process, and the benefits it brings to your Qt development workflow.

The Essence of the Qt Test Framework

Qt's Test framework is a lightweight and flexible testing solution designed specifically for Qt applications. It seamlessly integrates with Qt Creator, providing a convenient environment for writing, running, and managing your tests. The framework offers a rich set of macros and classes that simplify the creation of test cases, assertions, and test fixtures, empowering you to automate the verification of your code's correctness and robustness.

Key Components

The Qt Test framework comprises several key components that facilitate the testing process:

1. **Test Cases**: Test cases are the individual units of testing, each focusing on a specific aspect or functionality of your code. They are implemented as C++ classes that inherit from `QObject` and contain one or more test functions.
2. **Test Functions**: Test functions are the heart of your test cases, containing the actual code that exercises your application's functionality and verifies its behavior. They are decorated with the `Q_OBJECT` macro and the `private slots` specifier, allowing them to be executed by the Qt Test framework.
3. **Assertions**: Assertions are statements that express expectations about the behavior of your code. Qt's Test framework provides

various assertion macros, such as `QCOMPARE`, `QVERIFY`, and `QEXPECT_FAIL`, which evaluate conditions and report failures if the expectations are not met.
4. **Test Fixtures**: Test fixtures are optional classes that provide setup and teardown functionality for your test cases. They allow you to initialize data, create objects, or establish preconditions before each test function is executed, and clean up resources or restore the environment after each test.

Creating and Running Tests

To create and run tests using the Qt Test framework, follow these steps:

1. **Create a Qt Test Project**: In Qt Creator, choose the "Qt Test Project" template to create a new project specifically for your tests.
2. **Add Test Cases**: Within your test project, create C++ classes that inherit from `QObject` and contain your test functions.
3. **Write Test Functions**: Implement your test functions, using assertion macros to verify the behavior of your code.

4. **Build and Run**: Build your test project and execute it within Qt Creator. The Qt Test framework will automatically discover and run your test cases, reporting the results in the "Test Results" pane.

Example

Let's illustrate the creation of a simple test case:

C++

```
#include <QtTest/QtTest>

class MyTestClass : public QObject
{
    Q_OBJECT

private slots:
    void testAddition() {
        int result = 3 + 5;
        QCOMPARE(result, 8);
    }

    void testSubtraction() {
        int result = 10 - 4;
        QCOMPARE(result, 6);
    }
};
```

```
QTEST_MAIN(MyTestClass)
#include "mytestclass.moc"
```

In this example, we define a test class `MyTestClass` with two test functions: `testAddition()` and `testSubtraction()`. Each test function uses the `QCOMPARE` macro to verify that the results of simple arithmetic operations match the expected values.

Benefits of Testing

Incorporating the Qt Test framework into your development workflow offers several benefits:

- **Early Bug Detection**: Tests help identify errors and regressions early in the development process, reducing the cost and effort of fixing them later.
- **Code Confidence**: A comprehensive suite of tests provides confidence in the correctness and reliability of your code, enabling you to make changes and refactor with peace of mind.

- **Regression Prevention**: Tests act as a safety net, preventing the reintroduction of previously fixed bugs or unintended side effects of new code.
- **Documentation and Understanding**: Well-written tests serve as executable documentation, clarifying the intended behavior of your code and facilitating understanding for other developers.

The Qt Test framework empowers you to automate the verification of your code, ensuring its correctness, robustness, and maintainability. By creating and executing unit tests, you can catch errors early, build confidence in your code, and foster a culture of quality in your Qt development process. Embrace the power of testing, and let it guide you towards building reliable and high-quality Qt applications.

Chapter 19: Building Your Qt Developer Career

Creating a Portfolio

In the competitive landscape of software development, a well-crafted portfolio serves as your digital showcase, highlighting your skills, experience, and passion for Qt development. It's a tangible representation of your capabilities, allowing potential employers or clients to assess your expertise and envision the value you can bring to their projects. In this section, we'll delve into the art of creating a compelling Qt developer portfolio, exploring the key elements, project selection strategies, and presentation techniques that will leave a lasting impression and open doors to exciting opportunities.

The Essence of a Qt Developer Portfolio

A Qt developer portfolio is more than just a collection of projects; it's a curated showcase of your best work, demonstrating your proficiency in Qt, C++, and GUI development. It should tell a story about your skills, your passion, and your potential to contribute to the Qt ecosystem.

Your portfolio should be:

- **Relevant**: Focus on projects that showcase your Qt expertise and align with your career goals.
- **Diverse**: Include a variety of projects that demonstrate your versatility and ability to tackle different challenges.
- **High-quality**: Ensure that your projects are well-designed, functional, and visually appealing.
- **Well-documented**: Provide clear and concise descriptions of each project, highlighting your contributions and the technologies used.
- **Easily accessible**: Make your portfolio available online, preferably on a personal website or a platform like GitHub or GitLab.

Project Selection: Showcasing Your Best Work

Choosing the right projects for your portfolio is crucial. Aim for a balance between personal projects that showcase your passion and professional projects that demonstrate your experience. Consider the following:

- **Complexity and Scope**: Include projects that vary in complexity and scope, showcasing your ability to handle both small and large-scale Qt applications.

- **Technical Skills**: Highlight projects that demonstrate your proficiency in various Qt modules, such as Qt Core, Qt GUI, Qt QML, Qt Network, or Qt 3D.
- **Problem-Solving Abilities**: Choose projects that illustrate your problem-solving skills and your ability to overcome challenges in Qt development.
- **Creativity and Innovation**: Showcase projects that demonstrate your creativity and your ability to think outside the box.
- **Collaboration**: If you've worked on team projects, highlight your contributions and your ability to collaborate effectively with others.

Presentation: Making a Lasting Impression

The way you present your portfolio can significantly impact its effectiveness. Consider the following presentation techniques:

- **Clear and Concise Descriptions**: Provide a brief overview of each project, highlighting its purpose, key features, and your specific contributions.
- **Visuals and Screenshots**: Include screenshots or videos that showcase the

visual aspects and user experience of your projects.
- **Code Samples**: If appropriate, provide snippets of your code that demonstrate your clean coding style and understanding of Qt best practices.
- **Live Demos**: If possible, host live demos of your projects online, allowing potential employers or clients to interact with your creations and experience their functionality firsthand.
- **Personal Touch**: Infuse your personality into your portfolio, showcasing your passion for Qt development and your unique perspective.

Additional Portfolio Elements

Beyond showcasing projects, consider including the following elements in your portfolio:

- **Skills and Expertise**: List your technical skills and areas of expertise in Qt development, highlighting your proficiency in specific modules or technologies.
- **Education and Certifications**: Include information about your educational background and any relevant certifications you've earned.

- **Work Experience**: If you have prior professional experience in Qt development, provide a brief overview of your roles and responsibilities.
- **Contact Information**: Make it easy for potential employers or clients to reach out to you by providing your contact details, such as email address, phone number, or social media links.

Creating a compelling Qt developer portfolio is an investment in your career, showcasing your skills, experience, and passion to potential employers or clients. By carefully selecting projects, crafting clear and concise descriptions, and utilizing effective presentation techniques, you can build a portfolio that stands out, leaves a lasting impression, and opens doors to exciting opportunities in the world of Qt development..

Preparing for Interviews

In the pursuit of your dream Qt developer role, the interview process stands as a crucial gateway to showcasing your skills, knowledge, and passion to potential employers. While a well-crafted portfolio lays the foundation, thorough preparation is key to navigating interviews with confidence and leaving a lasting impression. In this section, we'll explore essential strategies and techniques for preparing for Qt developer interviews, empowering you to present your best self, articulate your expertise, and secure the job opportunities you desire.

Technical Preparation: Sharpening Your Qt Skills

A strong foundation in Qt concepts and best practices is paramount for success in technical interviews. Review the core Qt modules, such as Qt Core, Qt GUI, Qt QML, and Qt Network, ensuring a deep understanding of their functionalities and applications. Brush up on C++ programming fundamentals, including object-oriented programming, data structures, and algorithms, as these skills are often intertwined with Qt development.

Consider the following technical preparation strategies:

- **Review Qt Documentation**: Qt's comprehensive documentation is a treasure trove of knowledge. Revisit the documentation for the Qt modules relevant to your target roles, refreshing your

understanding of key classes, functions, and concepts.
- **Practice Coding Challenges**: Solve Qt-specific coding challenges or practice implementing common GUI elements or functionalities to hone your problem-solving skills and coding proficiency.
- **Explore Open-Source Qt Projects**: Analyze the codebase of open-source Qt projects to gain insights into real-world Qt development practices, architectural patterns, and coding styles.
- **Stay Updated with Qt Trends**: Keep abreast of the latest Qt developments, new features, and industry trends by following Qt blogs, forums, and social media channels.

Behavioral Preparation: Showcasing Your Soft Skills

Beyond technical expertise, employers also seek candidates with strong soft skills, such as communication, teamwork, and problem-solving abilities. Prepare to answer behavioral interview questions that assess these skills and demonstrate your fit within the company culture.

Consider the following behavioral preparation strategies:

- **Practice Common Interview Questions**: Research common behavioral interview questions and practice your responses, focusing on highlighting specific examples from your past experiences that demonstrate your skills and achievements.
- **Reflect on Your Strengths and Weaknesses**: Identify your key strengths and areas for improvement, and be prepared to articulate them honestly and constructively during the interview.
- **Research the Company and Position**: Gain a deep understanding of the company's mission, values, and culture, as well as the specific requirements and responsibilities of the Qt developer role you're applying for.
- **Prepare Questions to Ask**: Demonstrate your interest and engagement by preparing thoughtful questions to ask the interviewer about the company, the team, and the role itself.

Mock Interviews: Simulating the Real Experience

Conducting mock interviews with friends, mentors, or career coaches can be invaluable in refining your interviewing skills and boosting your confidence. Simulate the interview environment, practice answering questions under pressure, and receive feedback on your communication style, body language, and overall presentation.

Additional Tips

- **Dress Professionally**: Make a positive first impression by dressing appropriately for the interview.
- **Arrive Early**: Arrive at the interview location a few minutes early to allow time for settling in and collecting your thoughts.
- **Be Enthusiastic and Engaged**: Demonstrate your passion for Qt development and your eagerness to contribute to the company's success.
- **Follow Up**: Send a thank-you note to the interviewer after the interview, expressing your appreciation for their time and reiterating your interest in the position.

Preparing for Qt developer interviews involves a combination of technical and behavioral readiness. By sharpening your Qt skills, practicing common interview questions, researching the company and position, and conducting mock interviews, you can approach interviews with confidence and increase your chances of success. Remember, the interview is not just an assessment of your skills; it's also an opportunity to showcase your passion, personality, and potential to contribute to the company's growth. Embrace the challenge, prepare diligently, and let your Qt expertise shine through.

Navigating the Job Market

The journey of a Qt developer doesn't end with acquiring technical skills and crafting an impressive portfolio. It extends into the dynamic and ever-evolving landscape of the job market, where opportunities abound for those who are prepared and proactive. In this section, we'll explore the strategies and tactics for navigating the Qt job market, empowering you to identify promising opportunities, showcase your expertise, and secure the fulfilling and rewarding career you envision.

Embrace Continuous Learning

The world of technology is in a perpetual state of flux, with new frameworks, tools, and paradigms emerging at a rapid pace. As a Qt developer, embracing continuous learning is not just an option; it's a necessity. Stay abreast of the latest Qt developments, explore emerging trends, and expand your skillset to remain competitive and adaptable in the job market.

Consider the following strategies for continuous learning:

- **Qt Documentation and Resources:** Delve into Qt's official documentation, tutorials, and examples to deepen your understanding of the framework's capabilities and best practices.
- **Online Courses and Workshops**: Enroll in online courses or workshops that focus on advanced Qt topics, industry-specific applications, or emerging technologies that complement your Qt skills.
- **Open-Source Projects**: Contribute to open-source Qt projects to gain hands-on experience, collaborate with other developers, and showcase your skills to the community.
- **Conferences and Meetups**: Attend Qt-related conferences and meetups to network with fellow developers, learn from industry experts, and stay informed about the latest trends.

Building Your Network

Networking plays a vital role in career advancement, opening doors to hidden opportunities and fostering valuable connections within the Qt community. Cultivate relationships with fellow developers, industry professionals, and potential employers by:

- **Engaging in Online Communities**: Participate in Qt forums, discussion groups, and social media channels to share knowledge, seek advice, and connect with other Qt enthusiasts.
- **Attending Industry Events**: Network with professionals at Qt conferences, meetups, or other industry events to expand your connections and learn about potential job openings.
- **Reaching Out to Mentors**: Seek guidance and mentorship from experienced Qt developers who can offer valuable insights and career advice.

Job Search Strategies

When searching for Qt developer roles, adopt a proactive and targeted approach:

- **Online Job Boards**: Explore popular job boards and specialized Qt job platforms to discover relevant openings.
- **Company Websites**: Visit the career pages of companies known for their use of Qt to identify potential opportunities.
- **Networking and Referrals**: Leverage your network to uncover unadvertised positions or gain introductions to hiring managers.
- **Recruiters and Agencies**: Partner with recruiters or agencies specializing in Qt development to access a wider range of job opportunities.

Tailoring Your Resume and Cover Letter

Craft a compelling resume and cover letter that highlight your Qt expertise and align with the specific requirements of each job application. Tailor your documents to showcase relevant skills, projects, and accomplishments, demonstrating your value proposition to potential employers.

Acing the Interview

The interview is your opportunity to shine, showcasing your technical skills, problem-solving abilities, and passion for Qt development. Prepare thoroughly by reviewing Qt concepts, practicing common interview questions, and researching the company and position. During the interview, be confident, articulate, and enthusiastic, demonstrating your eagerness to contribute to the company's success.

Negotiating Your Offer

Once you receive a job offer, carefully evaluate its terms and conditions, including salary, benefits, and growth opportunities. Don't hesitate to negotiate to ensure the offer aligns with your expectations and market value. Seek advice from mentors or career coaches if needed.

Navigating the Qt job market requires a proactive and strategic approach. By embracing continuous learning, building your network, utilizing effective job search strategies, and preparing diligently for interviews, you can position yourself for success and secure a fulfilling and rewarding career as a Qt developer. Remember, your journey doesn't end with landing a job; it's a continuous process of growth, learning, and contributing to the vibrant Qt community.

Glossary of Key Teams

3D Graphics: The use of computer technology to create and manipulate three-dimensional images and animations.

Accessibility: The design of products, devices, services, or environments so that people with disabilities can access and use them.

Aspect: In Qt 3D, an aspect provides additional functionalities to a 3D scene, such as physics simulations, animation control, or audio playback.

Asynchronous Operations: Operations that do not block the execution of the main thread, allowing the user interface to remain responsive while the operation is performed in the background.

Base Class: In object-oriented programming, a base class is a class from which other classes (derived classes) inherit properties and methods.

Best Practices: Recommended methods or techniques that have proven to be effective and efficient in achieving desired outcomes.

Blocking Operations: Operations that halt the execution of the current thread until they are completed, potentially causing the user interface to freeze.

Build System: A collection of tools and processes used to compile and link source code into an executable application. Qt supports various build systems, including qmake and CMake.

C++: A high-performance, general-purpose programming language widely used for system-level programming, game development, and GUI applications.

Class: In object-oriented programming, a class serves as a blueprint or template for creating objects, defining their properties (data) and methods (behavior).

Client-Server Architecture: An architectural pattern in networked applications where clients initiate requests to a central server, which processes the requests and sends back responses.

Coding Conventions: A set of guidelines and best practices for formatting, naming, and structuring code to ensure consistency, readability, and maintainability.

Compiler: A software tool that translates human-readable source code into machine-executable code.

Component: In Qt 3D, a component defines the properties and behaviors of an entity within a 3D scene.

Context Property: A property that is accessible within a specific QML context, allowing data or functionality to be shared between QML and C++.

Cross-platform Development: The practice of developing software that can run on multiple operating systems or platforms with minimal or no code modifications.

Custom Delegate: A specialized component in Qt's Model-View architecture that controls the rendering and editing of individual data items within a view.

Custom Layout: A layout manager in Qt that is created by subclassing the `QLayout` class and implementing custom logic for widget arrangement and resizing.

Custom Signal: A user-defined signal in Qt that can be emitted from a `QObject`-derived class to notify other objects about events or state changes.

Custom Slot: A user-defined slot in Qt that can be connected to signals, enabling objects to respond to events and execute corresponding actions.

Custom Widget: A user-defined widget in Qt that extends the functionality or appearance of existing widgets or creates entirely new GUI elements.

Dangling Pointer: A pointer that points to a memory location that has been deallocated or is no longer valid, potentially leading to undefined behavior and crashes.

Data Race: A condition in multithreaded programming where multiple threads access and modify the same data concurrently, potentially leading to data corruption or inconsistencies.

Database Backend: The underlying database system used to store and manage data, such as SQLite, PostgreSQL, MySQL, or Oracle.

Database Driver: A software component that enables communication between your Qt application and a specific database backend.

Deadlock: A situation in multithreaded programming where two or more threads are blocked, each waiting for the other to release a resource, resulting in a standstill.

Debugging: The process of identifying, isolating, and resolving errors or defects within your code.

Declarative Language: A programming paradigm where you describe the desired outcome or behavior of your program rather than specifying the step-by-step instructions on how to achieve it. QML is a declarative language.

Delegate: In Qt's Model-View architecture, the delegate controls the rendering and editing of individual data items within a view.

Derived Class: In object-oriented programming, a derived class is a class that inherits properties and methods from a base class.

Design Patterns: Reusable solutions to common problems in software design, promoting code reusability, maintainability, and scalability.

Encapsulation: The bundling of data and the methods that operate on that data within a single unit (a class), protecting the data from unauthorized access and modification.

Entity: In Qt 3D, an entity represents an object within a 3D scene.

Error Handling: The process of anticipating, detecting, and gracefully handling errors or exceptional conditions within your code.

Event-Driven Programming: A programming paradigm where the flow of the program is determined by events, such as user input, sensor readings, or network messages.

Exception Handling: A mechanism in C++ for handling exceptional situations or errors by throwing and catching exceptions.

GUI (Graphical User Interface): A visual interface that allows users to interact with a computer or application through graphical elements like windows, buttons, and menus.

HTTP (Hypertext Transfer Protocol): The foundation of the World Wide Web, enabling the exchange of data between clients and servers.

Inheritance: An object-oriented programming concept that allows you to create new classes (derived classes) based on existing classes (base classes), inheriting their properties and methods.

Integrated Development Environment (IDE): A software application that provides comprehensive facilities to computer programmers for software development, typically consisting of a source code editor, build automation tools, and a debugger. Qt Creator is the IDE for Qt development.

Layout Manager: A component in Qt that arranges and manages the size and position of widgets within a window or container.

Memory Leak: A situation where dynamically allocated memory is not properly deallocated, leading to a gradual accumulation of unused memory and potential performance degradation or crashes.

Meta-Object Compiler (MOC): A Qt tool that processes QML and C++ code, generating additional code to support signals, slots, and other meta-object features.

Model: In Qt's Model-View architecture, the model represents the underlying data structure, providing data to views for presentation and handling data modification requests.

Model-View Architecture: A software architectural pattern that separates the concerns of data management (model), data presentation (view), and user interaction.

Multithreading: The ability of an operating system to execute multiple threads concurrently, potentially utilizing multiple processor cores for improved performance.

Mutex: A synchronization primitive that provides exclusive access to a shared resource, preventing multiple threads from accessing or modifying it simultaneously.

Networked Application: An application that communicates with other devices or services over a network.

Object: In object-oriented programming, an object is an instance of a class, representing a concrete entity in your program with its own set of properties and methods.

Object-Oriented Programming (OOP): A programming paradigm that revolves around the concept of objects, which encapsulate data and behavior.

Observer Pattern: A design pattern where objects can register their interest in specific events or state changes and receive notifications when those events occur.

Offline Installer: A Qt installer that contains all the necessary files for installation, making it suitable for environments with limited internet connectivity.

Online Installer: A Qt installer that downloads the required components during the installation process, typically resulting in a smaller download size.

Open-source Edition: The freely available edition of Qt, licensed under the GPLv3 or LGPLv3 licenses.

Overloaded Signals and Slots: The ability to define multiple signals or slots with the same name but different parameter lists within a class, enabling handling of different event variations.

Polymorphism: An object-oriented programming concept that allows objects of different classes to be treated as objects of a common base class.

Property Binding: A mechanism in QML that establishes dynamic relationships between properties, enabling elements to react and adapt to changes in their environment or user interactions.

Qt: A cross-platform application development framework widely used for creating GUI applications, embedded systems, and mobile apps.

Qt 3D: A module in Qt that provides a framework for creating, rendering, and interacting with 3D scenes within Qt applications.

Qt Creator: The integrated development environment (IDE) specifically designed for Qt development.

Qt Designer: A visual design tool within Qt Creator for creating and designing user interfaces.

Qt Network Module: A module in Qt that provides classes and functions for network programming, enabling communication over various protocols like HTTP, TCP, and UDP.

Qt Quick: A declarative UI framework within Qt that utilizes QML for designing fluid and dynamic user interfaces.

Qt Quick Controls: A collection of pre-built UI elements that seamlessly integrate with Qt Quick, providing essential components for building user interfaces.

Qt SQL Module: A module in Qt that provides classes and functions for database integration, enabling seamless interaction with various database backends.

Qt Test Framework: A framework within Qt for creating and executing unit tests to automate the verification of code correctness and robustness.

QML (Qt Modeling Language): A declarative language used in Qt Quick for designing user interfaces.

Race Condition: A situation in multithreaded programming where the behavior of a program depends on the relative timing or interleaving of multiple threads, potentially leading to data corruption or inconsistencies.

Responsive Design: The practice of designing user interfaces that adapt gracefully to different screen sizes, resolutions, and input modalities, providing an optimal user experience across various devices.

Semaphore: A synchronization primitive that controls access to a shared resource, allowing a specified number of threads to access it concurrently.

Made in United States
Orlando, FL
26 January 2025